BEYOND THE DARKNESS

BEYOND THE DARKNESS

Cynthia A. Kubetin & James Mallory, M.D.

Rapha
PUBLISHING

Houston, Texas

WORD PUBLISHING
Dallas · London · Vancouver · Melbourne

*I would like to dedicate this book
first to my mother, Terry, who somehow
in all the confusion made me believe in myself
and gave me the courage to go on.
Second, to my daughter, Krystal, who gave me
an unconditional love that produced
healing in my soul.
Third, to my sister, Jonnie, who so many times
took care of me and taught me about life.
Finally, to all my friends who told their stories
so you could hold onto their hope
when you have none.*

Acknowledgments

I would like to thank Robert McGee for making the writing of this book possible. I am also grateful that he has heard and responded to the Lord's call and worked so diligently to provide me and other victims of sexual abuse the help needed to go beyond this darkness.

Also I would like to thank Marilyn McGee for providing the name of the book and many profound scriptures as she heard the Lord's quiet voice.

Contents*

---

* All chapters of this book except that identified as by Dr. James Mallory are the writing of Cindy Kubetin. In the chapters written by Cindy, any use of the pronouns *I, me, mine, my,* and *myself* refers to her, except where those words occur in quoted material or dialogue by other speakers.

List of Special Helps

Foreword
by Robert S. McGee

This book poignantly describes the devastating effects of child sexual abuse. The cries of these victims express feelings ranging from worthlessness to hopelessness to inappropriate guilt to rage. If the process described in these pages is followed, a person can be led to a new hope, centered on God's word and a proven course that brings healing. Psalm 147:3 (NASB) promises that the Lord "heals the brokenhearted, and binds up their wounds."

If you are in the position of being a friend or counselor to an abused person, this book will help you gain new understanding. You will learn how to be more helpful and how to avoid some of the traps that can subvert the healing process.

If you have been or are an abuser, this book may help break through your denial and rationalizations as you read the devastating testimonies of sexually abused victims. Then you will have the possibility of repenting, stopping the abuse, and asking forgiveness. If you follow this course, then you will experience the wonder of God's healing and cleansing love.

If you have been abused, you will recognize that there are many who have gone through similar horrors. You will possibly experience many painful feelings and memories as you read about these kindred victims. If these feelings seem overwhelming or promote old destructive patterns (such as cutting, burning, bulimia, drinking, drugs, nightmares, flashbacks, promiscuity, accidents), then put the book aside. Call a trusted friend or counselor, get with a support group, seek help. When you are stabilized, read on, because there is definitely hope. The process described in these pages has proven over and over that a person can not only survive terrible travesties from the past, but can even learn to thrive.

Certain specific therapeutic techniques used by some specialists in this field to help reclaim memories and fuse fragments of memories and multiple personalities are not mentioned in detail. These approaches should be used only by experienced therapists specially trained in these areas. Also, people who have been abused in satanic or ritualistic settings should be treated only by experienced therapists who have worked in these areas. Failure to find professional help can result in these victims being overwhelmed with resurgent memories or suffering personality fragmentation which can lead to very destructive outcomes.

The authors' hopes and prayers for those of you who have been sexually abused are that you will make the transition from victim to survivor to thriver. Admittedly, the process can be slow, and it can include pain, setbacks, and frustrations. Yet the steps described in this book, along with the incredible power from the application of God's truths, are able to overcome any obstacle and bring hope and healing to the worst of situations. Be assured that "the Lord is near to the brokenhearted, and saves those who are crushed in spirit" (Ps. 34:18, NASB).

ROBERT S. MCGEE
President and Founder of Rapha

Houston, Texas
November 1991

A Note from Cindy

To my readers:

As you will learn in this book, God graciously restored me and took me beyond the darkness. For me it was a miracle of restoration to be asked to begin to tell my story in the same psychiatric ward where, with God's help and through my psychiatrist's urging, I had pieced together the hidden fragments of that story. Since then, God has been enabling me to work toward fulfilling my destiny by helping others emerge from the darkness into the light.

There is a "beyond" for you. You do have a purpose. Many of my clients requested that their stories be told so that perhaps your life would not suffer the consequences required of other victims. Many others expressed the desire for their stories to be shared so that you would know you were not alone in your despair. Still others wanted their stories to be told so that you could have hope. They wanted you to know they had victory in their lives.

Many men and women as well as my clients and I are praying that when you read this book, God will touch your life in such a way that you will be completely restored by His love. May God richly bless your recovery.

INTRODUCTION:

My Journey through the Darkness—
Cindy's Story

Five-year-old Susan had been in therapy for weeks, but until this particular session, little or no progress had been made. As she sat in my office, looking down to avoid eye contact, her large brown eyes had no light in them. She suddenly grasped a doll from the shelf and quickly removed its clothes. Finding another doll, she removed its pants and then placed it on top of the other. "This is what Daddy does to Carry," she sobbed, speaking of her eight-month-old sister. Her graphic description pointed to the life of darkness in which she and her sister were living.

In Susan's life, the tragic consequences of abuse were already evident, since she had been experiencing darkness for most of her life. In other cases, however, years may go by before the full, devastating impact of abuse is seen. The lingering effects of sexual abuse may vary, producing guilt, shame, anxiety, anger, and distrust in the victim. These emotions may, in turn, be manifested in such symptoms as withdrawal, depression, insomnia, memory blocks, panic attacks, and suicidal tendencies. Because memories are often repressed, a sexual abuse victim often cannot connect these symptoms with actual abuse or an abuser. When an abuse victim marries, she usually exhibits complicated behaviors in this new relationship. She may withdraw although she desperately wants to be held, or she may become cold and aggressive when she is shown love. She remains confused by her inability to achieve a deep, meaningful relationship with her husband, bonded by mutual love, trust, and respect. Being alone is terribly threatening, but being close terrifies her, too. She remains confused but desperate, craving intimacy while lacking hope that her attempts to receive it will be successful.

From the moment abuse occurs, the victim may lose objectivity. Her thinking becomes confused as she is overwhelmed by her feelings of guilt and her subsequent loss of self-respect. She tends to assume personal responsibility for the abuse, often making comments such as "I should have just stayed home," "I should have tried to fight back," "I should have told someone what was happening," or as in the case of date rape, "I shouldn't have been so friendly and open," "I must have given him the impression that I *wanted* to have sex," or "I shouldn't have gone out with him—where was my better judgment?" *Her* better judgment? The victim should—and needs—to return the responsibility of the abuse to the perpetrator.

Restoration is the goal of every sexual abuse victim. Because a mental and emotional death has taken place, the victim longs for a return to life. And restoration *can* take place, through God's power and the personal application of His truth. The victim then becomes more than a survivor; she is an overcomer, renewed by the hand of God.

Going beyond the Darkness Is Possible

From personal experience, I know that going beyond the darkness is possible. God has restored my life, which was clouded by sexual abuse. Isaiah 57:18 tells us God will make us whole by giving comfort, yet it took many years before I felt the comfort or received the wholeness.

As a very young child, I began to isolate myself from others because of sexual abuse. As is quite common, the very person whom I loved and believed was there for me was also my abuser. My memory is too sketchy for me to be sure of the extent of the abuse I was subjected to before I was seven, or whether there was more than one perpetrator in those early years. I do know that, including voyeurs and exhibitionists, there were at least ten perpetrators in my life by the time I reached adulthood. I also know that some of the traits I demonstrated indicated that I had been greatly traumatized at an early age.

Even when I was a very young child, I felt I could tell absolutely no one what was happening to me. Everyone around me had so many problems that I knew it would be useless. Besides, I loved my perpetrator. When he would come home from work, I would run out to meet him. Caught in this impossible situation, I chose to keep the abuse to myself and hide from others. It was a family joke that I would walk around the house with a towel over my head. I would, of course, run into things. The story goes that when I would encounter an obstacle, I would back up and go another direction. I remember that I could see just enough to make out people shapes, but I didn't want anyone to see me, and I didn't want to see.

I never played with children in the neighborhood. It just seemed safer to stay away from everyone. Trying to figure out if there were "good" persons around me kept me too confused.

I also remember always feeling sad, dirty, and completely alone. People frightened me. Once I lived in a place where the mothers in the neighborhood tried to be friendly and talk to me. I would run from them, wondering, *What do they want from me?* One in particular would leave me cookies, showing me from a distance that they were at her door, then going back inside her house. When I was sure she wasn't coming back outside, I would run as fast as I could to get them. I was so afraid and anxious, it seemed like miles down her walkway.

My mother finally took me to the psychiatrist to find out why I would not talk. I was trembling so hard on the inside I was sure the doctor could tell. The room seemed too white and too bright. The doctor seemed too powerful—I thought he must be mean. After a few visits he decided that I was perfectly all right, that I just didn't want to talk. He told my mother that whenever I got ready to, I would talk.

During this time in my life, I remember sometimes being put in a closet with the lights out and left there; at other times I would be put in a drawer. Sometimes I would be strapped to the toilet for several hours, and my legs would turn slightly blue. The reason for the strong punishment was that I was well past the age of being potty-trained but hadn't accomplished this task.

The worst part was feeling very alone and very afraid. Somehow I got enough strength to believe that all this didn't matter and that if I would be very still, or if I would hold my breath or count, I would get out of the closet or out of the drawer and everything would be okay. I wanted desperately to run, but I knew I couldn't. I'm not sure if the closet was locked or not; I just knew it was dark and I couldn't come out. Being crammed into the drawer was uncomfortable and hurt a little, but not bad. All this made me very angry and very sad, but most of all I just felt emptiness, an emptiness bigger than me. And I was sure that if I wasn't careful, the emptiness would swallow me up. So I just had to wait.

I finally became potty-trained, but the chaos in my life seemed to increase. I began to have horrible nightmares, filled with horrible monsters, half-men and half-horses. Every night they would come, and it was terrifying. I never even tried to tell anyone because everyone was so busy. I would go to the kitchen, move the canned goods around in the cabinet, and climb inside. I would think, *Tonight when they come I can hide in here since there is plenty of room.* I would also move enough items around to leave room for my mother to get into the cabinet with me where the monster couldn't hurt her.

Later I moved into a new family system, but there was still no safety for me. I continued to keep to myself, play by myself, and as much as I could, stay detached from everyone and everything.

Your story may have different details from mine. But if you are a victim from a dysfunctional family, you no doubt received the same messages I did: *Don't feel. Don't share. Don't be you. Don't risk. Don't trust. Don't get close. Don't be intimate. Don't—whatever you do—let anyone know who you are.*

As much as I wanted to please everybody around me by not calling attention to my feelings, I had to accept the fact that I was lonely and miserable in my isolation. I needed God. I needed people. I needed love. I needed intimacy.

Overcoming Denial

It took me years to finally fix vividly in my mind that I had been a victim. Somehow it seemed to me that the abuses had just happened to me, that this was a part of my life but that I really wasn't a victim. Even in the first therapy that I had at eighteen, no one said I had been victimized, or even that he was sorry those things had happened to me. When I actually recognized that I had been a victim of child molestation, I was devastated. I felt more shame than ever. My flashbacks became more frequent, and I felt despicable and worthless. As God's restorative power began to take hold of me, however, I not only saw myself as a victim, but also that it was possible to become a survivor.

When I was in a state of denial, I couldn't picture myself as either victim or survivor. But as time passed, I began to think of myself more and more often as a survivor. I even began to feel a joy in having lasted through so much. I saw more positive things about myself than I ever had, and even learned to risk myself a little more.

I liked this stage, but there was still too much pain inside, too much anxiety and fear. Also, I continued making grave mistakes in my life. It was obvious to me that I didn't yet have it all together.

By this time, I had begun really to seek God in my life. I wanted the mental torment to stop, not just for a day, but for a lifetime. But when I would read all the Bible's wonderful scriptures, I was sure that they applied to some great mission of God; surely this book couldn't have been written to help me. To see the Bible as an instrument of beautifully tuned words that produce life when played wasn't yet possible for me. I hadn't begun to understand the way of Jesus, that His path was for me to have the good things of life, not the bad things; that He wanted to redeem my life. But I kept reading, and for me, verses 4 and 5 of Psalm 103 (NASB) explained the Lord's way quite well:

> Who redeems your life from the pit
> Who crowns you with lovingkindness and compassion
> Who satisfies your years with good things,
> So that your youth is renewed like the eagle.

As I read these words my heart pounded with hope. It was still difficult to believe, but I knew that even a little faith was better than none. God said He would renew my youth "like an eagle" and satisfy my years with good things. He said He would redeem me and make my life different.

A Cry to God

Even with this assurance in my heart, the recovery years were a struggle, with little evidence of progress. Surely there had to be more to life than I was experiencing. In anger one day, I cried out to God, "Help me!" He responded by making clear to me the principle of restoration as found in Genesis and by giving me a role model in the story of Joseph. I pray this passage will be helpful to you as well.

The gripping story of Joseph and his twelve brothers is found in chapters 37–50 of Genesis. Joseph, the youngest of the boys, and favorite of his father, was the target of intense jealousy from his brothers. Fearing for Joseph's safety, the father, Jacob, would not allow Joseph to travel with the older boys to pasture a flock of sheep in the city of Shechem. Yet, some time later Joseph was sent to check on their welfare and progress. The brothers were found near the city of Dothan, a name whose literal translation is "double sickness," a phrase that perfectly describes my feelings of being sexually abused. To me, being abused was more than a sickness; rather it was a double sickness, a constant pain deep inside me and a dark despair from which there seemed to be no escape. And even after the abuse stopped, that gnawing two-pronged sickness continued to live and grow in my body.

Near Dothan, Joseph's brothers threw him into a pit. He begged his brothers not to go on with this thing they were doing to him. Almost every victim of sexual abuse pleads with the perpetrator at some time to stop what is being done to him or her. For me, being abused was like being thrown into a pit—a pit so deep I couldn't get out of it and in which I was going to die.

What I Learned from Joseph

Joseph's brothers sold him to a caravan of Ishmaelites. It is interesting that the Hebrew word *Ishmael* means "God will hear," for on this journey, Joseph must have surely cried out to God for help, as most victims do. Perhaps he was comforted with the thought "God will hear," as I was. "When, O God, when?" I also cried.

When Joseph reached Egypt, he was sold to Potiphar, an officer of Pharaoh. To learn that the name *Potiphar*, in the Hebrew, means "my affliction was broken," heightened the identification with Joseph that I had begun to feel, for my affliction had been broken and the abuse had stopped. But, just like Joseph, I was still a prisoner—in my mind. I felt shame and guilt. I felt worthless and dirty.

As I continued to follow the story of Joseph, I learned that his life became worse and that he was again victimized, thrown into prison for no sin of his own. I looked at my own life and saw how I too had been revictimized, repeatedly.

But I also saw that Joseph had God's favor. Even in the midst of his imprisonment, he was promoted to leadership, and the jail setting proved to be a learning ground for his future role as ruler in Egypt. I decided to approach my life in a different way and try the concept of using my circumstances right now to the fullest. Perhaps, like Joseph, I had been given this time to prepare for something greater. I could learn how to live, how to feel, how to love.

Joseph eventually was taken out of prison and elevated to second in command of Egypt, a position similar to that which he would have had in Israel with his father, Jacob. The Pharaoh gave him a wife, and she and Joseph had a son they named Manasseh, meaning "God has made me forget." As I read this passage, I began to cry. All my life I had wanted to forget what had happened to me, but I just hadn't known how. I had seen and felt God's restoration in certain areas of my life already, but that day I was truly understanding Him.

God made Joseph forget the pain, the anger, the loneliness, and all the other distressing emotions he must have felt. I was not through my journey as a Joseph, but now I had the direction: restoration—restoration from all the hurt! I was, over a period of time, to become whole; I was to live again.

Now I understood that I couldn't run away from the darkness, and I realized that I couldn't fix the darkness. I saw that the surpassing greatness of God would shine the light into the darkness. I had been afflicted, but I wasn't crushed. I was perplexed, but not desolate and void of hope. I had been persecuted, but not forsaken; struck down, but not destroyed. I was a survivor.

From Surviving to Overcoming

I wanted more. It disturbed me that sometimes I would flip back to being a victim, although my hope was real by this time and the treasure I had was inside. Even when I was afflicted and struck down again, I knew I wasn't destroyed and that I was different. I took heart from Romans 12:2: "And do not be conformed to this world, but be transformed by the renewing of your mind, that you may prove what is that good and acceptable and perfect will of God" (NKJV). I had hope for this renewal in my life.

I knew that this scripture would also be a part of my healing process. It was telling me not to be fashioned or shaped by my own experiences of sexual abuse, which cause me to be unstable, but to be changed by letting God make me new again. By overcoming what the world had done to me, the victory in my life would be witness that the will of God is good and acceptable and perfect.

I knew then that God had not used sexual abuse to "teach me some profound lesson." The Old Testament records that God had set the death penalty for this crime. He was showing me that His will was to restore my life from that which had been stolen by the abuse. I began to be restored.

I had believed all my life in the lies I had heard, and now I was trying to believe in the truth: that Jesus was the son of God; that I was born of God; and that God had victory over the evils of the world.

I wanted to be like Caleb when he quieted the people of Israel in their impatience to enter the Promised Land ". . . and [Caleb] said, We should by all means go up and take possession of [the promised land], for we shall surely overcome it" (Num. 13:30, NASB). I wanted to believe that God was with me as He was when He spoke with Joshua, ". . . Be strong and courageous! Do not tremble or be dismayed, for the Lord your God is with you, wherever you go" (Josh. 1:9, NASB). I did tremble and become dismayed at times, but somewhere I found the courage to continue.

I know now that courage came from God, because even when I thought I couldn't go on with my recovery, I did. Even when I thought I couldn't deal with one more memory, I did. Even when I thought I couldn't pray one more prayer, I did.

The more I overcame, the more peace I experienced in my life. Sometimes it would seem that nothing was going on in my recovery process, but then I would notice that I could sleep peacefully at night, or that I didn't say I hated myself so often. I was like the Shunamite woman's son; I was being restored to life.

At about this same time, I began to realize that I no longer had allergies or colitis, and only occasionally had migraine headaches. As God promised in Jeremiah 30:17 to restore Israel to health, so my health was being restored. "'For I will restore you to health and I will heal you of your wounds,' declares the Lord, 'because they called you an outcast. . . .'" God truly was healing my hurts, my disappointments, my failures, my wounds, and I was no longer an outcast.

I didn't feel dirty any more. Also, I saw that other people no longer had the power to make me feel dirty. God had restored my dignity. I had changed. How could I now be affected by what people said, when I knew what God said? I was an overcomer. I was no longer broken. I felt no shame, no condemnation. God had given me back my innocence.

I was excited. There was a joy inside me that had never been there before, a belief that even when victory was delayed, I still had hope in God. Although I was uncertain about what was actually happening, I knew it was something wonderful and that I could now focus completely on getting on with my journey.

I had come far enough to know that the road to recovery was one that I must walk by myself. I read everything that I thought would help lift the state of depression that still hung over me. When I got impatient, thinking my progress was taking too much time, or discouraged about my ability to make it any farther, I would tell myself, "Tomorrow is another day," or "I will feel better. Tomorrow I will feel better." Saying the words again and again somehow always seemed to help me get through the day.

He has restored me and He can also restore your life. I have taken the risk of placing recovery in His hands, and I can assure you that He does bring healing and restoration from the pain and hurt of loss and abuse.

Later in this book I will share with you twelve steps God took me through in my recovery from sexual abuse. The world had offered only surviving, and that's what I did when I depended only on the world—I merely survived. I didn't commit suicide, but I ached inside everyday. But God offered restoration—a new life. He taught me that there was much more than surviving, that there was overcoming. I didn't have the twelve steps written out then, of course, but I've done so in chapter 7 so that you may use them in your own journey to recovery. I hope that reading these steps from time to time will give you direction and encouragement, as they did me.

Going "Beyond"

As I've shared in this chapter, God graciously restored me and took me beyond the darkness. Several years ago, I felt directed to speak, teach, and counsel. Much time passed and then one day, I was asked to speak on sexual abuse to a Christ-centered in-hospital Rapha unit. I was overwhelmed with joy, as my audience would be the directors, therapists, nurses, and staff of the very hospital where I had begun my recovery process from sexual abuse. To tell my story in the same psychiatric ward where with God's help, through my psychiatrist's urging, I had pieced together the hidden fragments of that story was for me a miracle of restoration. Truly He had not only restored me, but I was fulfilling my destiny, as I hope you will, as you make your own journey through the darkness and beyond.

CINDY KUBETIN

Houston, Texas
November 1991

1.
The Darkness—
A Definition

"When I expected good, then evil came;
When I waited for light, then the darkness came."
—Job 30:26, NASB

A sixty-seven-year-old man staying in a convalescent home describes the horror of what goes on at night. Speaking in not much more than a whisper as his own voice reflects the disbelief of the sexual harassments, he describes being exposed, viewed, and fondled. He keeps reassuring the listener that he's not crazy or drugged. "It really happened," he says, as he looks to the floor in great despair.

An adult victim describes her first experience of sexual abuse: "I was about eight, maybe nine years old. Mother had started working nights, so now it was Daddy who put me to bed. I began to feel uneasy when Daddy would come into the bathroom, but I didn't understand. I thought, *He's looking at me kind of strange*. One night he said he needed to look at me all over to see if I was growing all over. I felt funny, but when he began to hold me, it felt good to be so close. It felt real good to be held again, just like Mommy used to do. I didn't even mind too much when he touched me down there. After a while he got up and said he was sorry. He said he loved me very much.

"Everything seemed so strange, so confusing that night, but I liked having Daddy so close to me. I guess I felt special.

1

I went to sleep crying, but thinking, *Daddy really loves me*. The next night, or maybe it was the next time—it seems all confused now—Daddy didn't hold me so much. He looked a lot and touched me real hard. He breathed real hard, so hard I thought he might die. I was really scared, and I felt so helpless. I knew I must really be bad for this to happen to me. Daddy said he was sorry and wouldn't do it again. I didn't believe Daddy this time and I didn't feel special."

Genny, a forty-year-old outgoing blonde, describes a form of sexual abuse which is extremely harmful and commonly overlooked—visual sexual abuse.

"My stepfather never touched me, but he was always walking into the bathroom or my bedroom. He was always peeking, leering, or staring at me. I felt totally disgusted. I think I really hated him even more because he would act like it was an accident. When I would complain about him to my mom, she would say, 'I'll talk to him,' but nothing ever changed. My mom never even got the locks to the bathroom fixed."

In this instance in Genny's life, both parents were abusive. The effects of her stepfather's actions were obviously shame-producing and her mother's passivity only reinforced the pain and betrayal. Some people might want to discount this as sexual abuse, since no physical contact occurred. Yet Genny was sexually abused just as much as if she had been fondled. This type of sexual abuse produces the same effects as those found in the victim who has been touched.

Another victim in her late thirties explains that she doesn't enjoy sex with her husband and will do anything to avoid it. She is always very firm and clear about the issue of sexual abuse, emphasizing that she was never overtly sexually abused by anyone, and that, in fact, her father is a preacher. She further states that she loves her husband and is very grieved about this part of her life. However, there is one thing that has always bothered her. Her bedroom in one house she lived in as a child was next to her parents' room. Almost every night she would hear her mother sobbing, "Please don't make me do this. Stop! It hurts so bad. Please leave me alone." Then there would be silence, except for a faint crying.

Defining Sexual Abuse

Certainly, these episodes have produced consequences in the woman's life which, under the broad definition below, could be termed sexual abuse. The intent of this book is to define sexual abuse and encourage the victim in such a way that God's plan for the restoration of its victims can proceed.

Given the range of these stories, we can conclude that anyone can be a victim of sexual abuse. We can also conclude that any sexual activity carried out in an inappropriate context is abusive. A complete definition of sexual abuse, then, must be as broad as the range of human sexual activity. With a narrow definition both victims and perpetrators tend to minimize the harmful results, or even deny that sexual abuse has occurred.

Sexual abuse can be defined broadly as "any sexual activity, verbal, visual or physical, engaged in without consent, which may be emotionally or physically harmful and which exploits a person in order to meet another person's sexual or emotional needs. The person does not consent if he or she cannot reasonably choose to consent or refuse because of age, circumstances, level of understanding, and dependency or relationship to the offender."*

Verbal Sexual Abuse

We can define verbal sexual abuse as remarks including sexual threats, innuendoes, comments about a person's body, solicitation, harassment, coarse jesting, inappropriate sexual

---

*Robert S. McGee and Dr. Harry Schaumburg, *Renew: Hope for Victims of Sexual Abuse* (Houston: Rapha Publishing, 1990), p. 5.

talking, and sexual name-calling—any verbal expression with intent to arouse or stimulate. One woman told of being subjected to this kind of abuse by her family. Her stepmother would constantly tell her how the only thing her father wanted was sex and would describe her father as being dirty and vulgar and as wanting the stepmother to perform certain sexual acts. Then, when the father would arrive in the evening, the stepmother would provokingly seduce the father by rubbing up against his body in front of the daughter. The stepmother would then further engage in other seductive behaviors with the father.

Visual Sexual Abuse

Visual sexual abuse includes voyeurism, exhibitionism, viewing of pornographic material, of genitals, or of any sexual activity such as masturbation or intercourse. A teenager angrily describes the fear and revulsion she felt when her father took her to a XXX-rated movie theater to help her understand the facts of life. She says the worst thing that he ever did to her was to take her back to her house so they could watch through the window as her mother and her mother's boyfriend had sex.

Physical Sexual Abuse

Physical sexual abuse includes any inappropriate form of touching, from hugging to rape. Rubbing, holding, and kissing for the purpose of sexual gratification are examples. Also included in physical sexual abuse are oral, genital, anal, and breast stimulation, and penetration by penis, fingers, or any other body part or object, of mouth, anus, or vagina.

Most persons recognize inappropriate touching as sexual abuse, but sometimes denial still plays a part. For example, when a person has had a single experience of being fondled, he or she might discount the importance of this event. It is true some individuals who are otherwise emotionally sound might experience less of an impact in their lives than someone with less stability. But the important point is not to discount the effects that even one incident can produce in the life of a victim.

Ritualistic Sexual Abuse

The topic of ritualistic sexual abuse is of such overriding importance that a full chapter has been devoted to it. Please see chapter 2.

The Need for Recovery

Every victim, whether having experienced a one-time incident or multiple incidents, over a long or short period of time, needs to recover from the effects of the abuse. God truly wants to heal him or her so that nothing from the past will keep the victim from being a whole person in Christ. The point is to recover from any trauma in life.

Men are more likely than women to discount any sexual abuse in their childhood. One reason men discount abuse is that they do not like admitting to having been victims. A second reason is that often they are told that this is their first sexual experience. With the present double standard on sexual activity for men vs. women, men usually tend to agree with the proposal. A third reason, as with any victim, is the shame and guilt that he or she feels at being a victim of sexual abuse.

Sometimes victims are confused about whether they have been abused or not. Perhaps they have some vague memory from so long ago they don't know if it has any reality. No one can tell others with absolute certainty whether they have or have not been sexually abused. However, memory blocks are often a symptom of abuse having occurred.

Sherry describes her memory of abuse as "pictures and frames like in a film—dark and shadowy and only a moment of something bad happening." Another victim describes

flashbacks as bits and pieces of the past, but nothing clear—
"a man walking down the hall and someone standing in the
door—like a bad dream; or maybe it was a dream—who
really knows?"

Jan Frank, in her book on sexual abuse, *A Door of Hope*,*
encourages women to pray verse 6 of Psalm 51. This scripture
asks God for renewal of the innermost parts and for wisdom.
I encourage every victim of abuse to pray this prayer, that
with the help of God they will remember only that which is
important for recovery. Don't become bogged down in trying
to force yourself to remember things from the past. Allow
God to bring about insights and memories according to his
timing so you are not overwhelmed and can deal with them
one by one. But recovery is hard work and will sometimes
include remembering things we don't want to.

Signs and Symptoms of Sexual Abuse

In the next several pages you will find lists stating common
difficulties experienced by victims of sexual abuse. Not everyone who has these symptoms is a victim of sexual abuse,
of course. Nevertheless, if you are wrestling with several of
these symptoms, you might consider asking God to guide
you into restoration.

Many persons who have attempted recovery programs of
various types find that their lives are still in confusion. Others
have tried to do all the things people tell them to do and are
still in despair. Some deny that anything is wrong. Whatever
your circumstances, please review the list of signs and symptoms of sexual abuse on the next three pages and consider the
questions at the end of the chapter. The key to recovery is to
seek God's help regarding the truth about sexual abuse in
your life and to allow Him to guide you out of darkness, if that
is your condition.

---

*Jan Frank, *A Door of Hope* (San Bernardino, CA: Here's Life Publishers, Inc., 1987).

Possible Signs and Symptoms of Sexual Abuse in Children
(Toddlers, Preschool and School-age Children, Teenagers)

1. Nightmares
2. Withdrawal
3. Pseudo-maturity
4. Violent play
5. Low self-esteem
6. Fear of undressing
7. Stomach pain/headaches
8. Running away from home
9. Outbursts of anger
10. Early sexual promiscuity
11. Fear of being alone
12. Unprovoked crying spells
13 Sexually transmitted disease
14 Pregnancy or fear of pregnancy
15. Clinging to significant adult
16. Excessive bathing or brushing of teeth
17. Loss of appetite/increase in appetite
18. Refusal to go to school/leaving school
19. Fear of specific person(s), situation(s) or stranger(s)
20. Vaginal discharge/unusual odor in genital area
21. Seductive or sexual behavior with peers or adults
22. Bleeding, bruises, or problems walking or sitting
23. Pain, itching, redness on genitalia, vaginal, and anal area
24. Increase in activity level/decrease in attention span
25. Behavior problems at school/change in school performance

Possible Signs and Symptoms of Sexual Abuse in Female Victims

1. Secrecy
2. Suicidal thoughts, feelings, attempts
3. Depression
4. Promiscuous behavior
5. Insomnia
6. Distrust of authorities or of everyone
7. Memory blocks
8. Overly critical attitude
9. Guilt/shame
10. Low self-esteem
11. Self-destructive behavior
12. Eating disorders
13. Seductive behavior
14. Withdrawal/isolation of self from others
15. Perceived helplessness
16. Headaches/stomachaches
17. Inability to say no
18. Loss of self-control
19. Repeated victimization
20. Underachievement/overachievement
21. Panic attacks/anxiety attacks
22. Sexual detachment/sexual addiction
23. Difficulty in sustaining relationships
24. Difficulty in handling sexual relationships
25. Anger toward everyone/anger with children and spouse

Possible Signs and Symptoms of Sexual Abuse in Male Victims

1. Guilt
2. Shame
3. Anger
4. Anxiety
5. Self-hate
6. Depression
7. Stomachaches
8. Headaches
9. Withdrawal
10. Nervousness
11. Fear of abuser
12. Suicidal feelings
13. Confusion of identity
14. Low self-esteem
15. Feelings of betrayal
16. Secrecy/avoidance/denial
17. Adoption of "macho" persona
18. Discounting or minimizing of sexual experiences
19. Difficulty in disclosing abuse
20. Fear of adult men and/or women
21. Sexual overactivity/sexual underactivity
22. Sexual detachment/sexual addiction
23. Difficulty in interactions with adult friends
24. Confused feelings about sex/sex problems
25. Difficulty with feelings about sexual relationships

WORKBOOK

1. Do any of the listed effects of sexual abuse apply to you?
   Which ones?

2. In Job 30:26 (NASB), in his final statement of his case, Job
   says: "When I expected good, then evil came;/ When I
   waited for light, then the darkness came." What do those
   words mean to you?

3. How do you think sexual abuse has affected and currently affects your relationships with others?

4. Describe how you feel when you are called a victim.

5. Write out any flashbacks of sexual abuse that you have experienced. (Note: This question may be emotionally dangerous to do alone or without professional guidance. Don't force yourself to respond if doing so is too painful.)

6. Make a chart of the chronological time span of your life, showing any memory blocks.

7. List areas of your past about which you have no memory or whose memories are painful, and pray about them according to verse 6 of Psalm 51: "Sincerity and truth are what you require; fill me with your wisdom" (TEV).

8. Read Judges chapters 19 through 21. Based on these chapters, what do you think God's attitude toward rape is? How does that compare with contemporary society's attitude toward rape?

9. Describe your family in comparison to the husband in Judges 19.

10. Set and list here specific goals you want to reach in your recovery from sexual abuse.

2.

In Utter Darkness—
The Horror of Ritualistic Abuse

By James D. Mallory, Jr., M.D.

Ritualistic sex abuse represents the ultimate in human degradation, torture, mind control, and destructiveness to the innermost self. It is as if a new chamber in Pandora's box has been discovered and unlatched. The ensuing revelations seem unbelievable. In fact, the need to disbelieve such human degradation is very strong. It flies in the face of secular humanism's naive, optimistic beliefs, hopes, and ideals regarding mankind. It represents an evil so great that the door is open to face evil as a supernatural entity, and this also goes against humanism's antisupernatural bias. Experts in this field express considerable frustration over the prevailing attitude that such practices are nonexistent or very rare. Unfortunately, this level of denial extends to many educators, law enforcement personnel, and media personnel.

However, with increased openness about sex in general, more people are beginning to identify terrible abuses in these areas. In turn, these revelations have uncovered a pattern of response to such abuse so that knowledgeable therapists, doctors, educators, child care personnel, and pastors have a higher index of suspicion and are asking appropriate questions and making appropriate referrals. Thus, there is an escalating recognition that ritualistic sex abuse is not so isolated or so rare as once believed. The majority of the abusers are involved in satanic rituals and worship. Sometimes the abusers are the child's own parents who are involved in a subgroup of Satanists. Other cases of abuse have occurred without the parents' knowledge in virtually every setting where their children are entrusted to the care of others, be it in day-care centers, schools, pre-school, church, and camps, or with neighbors, babysitters, or special friends.

Components of Ritualistic Abuse

The abuse itself is devastating physically, sexually, psychologically, and spiritually. Physical abuse includes essentially every form of torture ever described including beatings, cuttings, tattooing, painful electrical shock to genitals, puncture wounds, injections, being hung in various positions, being deprived of water, food, and sleep, nearly drowning, being buried alive, and being forced to consume blood, feces, urine, or body parts. Ritualistic sexual abuse is degrading, sadistic, and painful. It includes multiple sexual attacks from members of the group, insertion of painful instruments in body orifices, forced sexual activity with animals, infants, or the dead.

Psychological abuse is designed to gain total control over the person. This is carried out by physical threats, coupled with actually carrying out some of the mentioned tortures. Victims are forced to engage in repulsive, often illegal activities and then told this has sealed their fate and they can never play any role in society again except as a cult member. They are brainwashed against family (if family is not a member of the cult) and church and society in general, with the desired result being that of forcing them to believe the only place they can exist is in the cult itself. Various mind-controlling techniques are utilized, such as food-, water-, and sleep-deprivation, long indoctrination sessions, use of drugs, threats, torture, and programming for specific destructive activities.

Spiritual abuse consists of forcing victims to participate in rituals, activities, and instructions that induce the belief that they are totally separated from God and are totally controlled by Satan. They are often told they have spirit demons that will control them and punish them if they fail to obey. And, of course, these people may, in fact, be under demonic influence. The younger a person is when ritual abuse begins, the greater the emotional damage and the likelihood of being indoctrinated and incorporated into the cult's beliefs and actions.

Signs and Symptoms of Ritual Abuse

Signs and symptoms that should raise suspicion of ritual abuse include special fears, dreams, preoccupations, behaviors, descriptions of peculiar events, and physical symptoms. Special fears include such themes as death, devils, demons, monsters, ghosts, being confined, being harmed, being kidnapped, something bad happening to family or them, or the presence of something bad or scary inside the person's body. Dreams or nightmares may include the same themes.

Preoccupations include body excrement and body functioning, body genitals, and the general fears mentioned above. Behaviors are sadistic and sexual toward others, animals, and toys. Victims may engage in strange songs or chants or in making various signs or marks that are reflective of the cult's rituals.

Children may describe unusual events at school, church, camp, or wherever the abuse is occurring. Suspicion should be aroused when children talk about special pills, drugs, candy, or shots they are getting. They may describe people in strange costumes doing strange or sexual things. Costumes may include those of benign TV characters or scary or devilish characters. Descriptions of photographs, nudity, or strange play with animals or adults should be taken very seriously.

Physical signs may be bleeding from the vagina or rectum or infection in these areas. Unexplained or strange pains, bruises, or markings on the body may be found. Such children are also very prone to a whole host of physiological symptoms such as headache, stomachache, bowel dysfunction, and sleep disturbance. Because of the extreme stress on the nervous system, virtually any so-called psychosomatic symptom—skin rashes, seizurelike episodes, dizziness, anesthesia in various parts of the body—may occur.

The Uncertain Prognosis

Without professional help, the outcome for these victims is very grim. Many become so brainwashed and indoctrinated that they remain in the cult as abusers themselves. Those who get away from the perpetrators and try to live a normal life are plagued with a host of physical, emotional, spiritual, and behavioral problems. These people are often treated for psychosomatic illnesses, hysteria, and other personality disorders, depression, phobias, panic attacks, obsessions, and schizophrenia. However, if the underlying trauma from the ritual abuse is not treated, they will never experience adequate healing. Unfortunately, the underlying trauma may not even be remembered. It may seem incredible that such horrible abuse could be forgotten. Ironically, the very mental mechanism that helps people survive this kind of trauma also can block conscious recall years later. This phenomenon is called dissociation.

The Phenomenon of Dissociation

If a person is overwhelmed with severe abuse, torture, or terror, particularly during childhood, the protective mechanism of dissociation may come into play. Such persons are able to assume an altered stated of consciousness in which they "dissociate" themselves from the agonizing event. It is as if they are somewhere else and the abuse is happening to a different person.

Dissociation may result in partial or total memory block.

More dramatic effects may result in a state of fugue, or flight, in which a person assumes a new identity and is totally unable to recall the previous one. Fugue is separate from multiple personality disorder, which is the usual outcome of severe childhood abuse and will be discussed in more detail later.

It should be noted that the ability to dissociate is not simply a pathological process. It actually protects the victim from being totally overwhelmed and nonfunctioning. However, for more complete healing to take place the dissociated memories and personalities must be recalled and integrated into the total personality.

Depersonalization

Other effects of dissociation include depersonalization and derealization. Depersonalization is a frightening experience, and the person is completely aware of what is taking place. It seems to such individuals that they are suddenly outside their body, as if they are observing some other person interacting with the environment. They may describe feeling as if they were in a dream or like a robot. There may also be a sense of no feeling in various parts of the body and not being in control of one's speech and behavior.

Derealization

Derealization is a phenomenon where the environment suddenly seems altered or dreamlike, but the person maintains his or her own sense of personal reality, unless depersonalization also occurs, which is not uncommon. Size and shape of things may change; people may seem to be robots or dead, or phantoms of some sort.

Multiple Personality Disorder

There has been at least a tenfold increase in reported sexual abuse in the past ten years. As therapists have become more alert to asking questions about such abuse, they are discovering that this is a much more common problem than originally thought. In spite of the heightened awareness of sexual abuse and its connection with multiple personality disorder (MPD), there is said to be a 6.8-year delay in making a diagnosis of multiple personality disorder after the person has come for help.*

The basic goal in treating multiple personality disorder is integration of the alter personalities (referred to hereafter as *alters*). It is important to keep in mind that we are dealing with one person who is made up of different personalities—or better, personality fragments. Each alter has special feelings, roles, and reactions, and each has developed a response to severe trauma. We must help the person to understand that even the most negative alters have positive aspects and, certainly, positive potential; thus the goal is not to get rid of a basic part, but rather to have a healthy integration so the positive traits of the different alters can add up to an improved whole. Hopefully, the negative traits can be dealt with so that they do not continue as a destructive force. The alters need to know they are a part of a larger whole which, under God, is good. The alters need to be engaged in a joint venture to bring health, wholeness, and harmony into the one person.

Engaging the alters in this type of joint venture requires the development of trust, a sense of safety, and specific ways of engaging alters in conversation.

Some MPD clients already know about some of the alters and can switch from one to the other on request, and sometimes the switch simply occurs spontaneously.

Unknown alters may come out as they perceive the therapist to be trustworthy and not harmful. Some may be reached only when the therapist helps the client achieve a relaxed

---

*Daniel W. Hardy, M.D., J.D., et al., "Multiple Personality Disorder: Failure to Diagnose and the Potential for Malpractice Liability," *Psychiatric Annals* 18:9 (September 1988) 543-47.

state and use guided imagery, such as walking through a home and finding different alters in different rooms. Asking alters to write or do artwork may reveal more about them and help them feel more understood; consequently, they will be more likely to reveal themselves in this joint venture of bringing health to the whole person.

It is important for alters to understand they are not separate persons. In MPD one person is made up of various alters, and each has something to contribute. The alters need to understand that harming another alter is in reality harming themselves, and that they will never be fully functioning until they come together into a better whole.

MPD represents a unique opportunity to bring healing at a significantly deep level. As each alter is revealed, engagement can be made in a way so that the experience is one of a good relationship, clear communications, and faulty ideas corrected, with the attendant release of powerful, hurtful emotions with new understanding which frees them from being dominated by such.

This healing process requires a therapist specifically trained and experienced in the MPD area. A person with MPD can be greatly harmed if, without the guidance and help of a specially trained therapist, powerful memory fragments and alters become a chaotic, overpowering experience.

Alters, and ultimately the integrated person, also need to have distortions about God corrected. In many noncultic abuse cases, the perpetrators claim to be Christian, so that some of the alters may be very hostile toward Christianity. Also, the person or a specific alter may feel abandoned by or separated from God for the abuse to have taken place in the first place. Such an individual needs a corrective experience of a loving, caring community, be it a therapy group or a group of Christians with whom he or she can share and pray. This person also needs to develop an enlightened understanding of the true gospel of grace, so he or she can experience God's saving, healing, loving, comforting power.

Many victims of sexual abuse who have developed MPD do not seek help for the condition or for dissociation and may be unaware of both. Instead, they seek help for depression, self-abusive behavior, low self-esteem, post-traumatic stress symptoms, a host of physical symptoms, difficulty establishing and maintaining relationships, sexual dysfunction, and eating disorders.* Additional symptoms include migraine headaches, hearing voices, amnesia, and visual distortions such as objects appearing very small.**

The Healing Process

The general process of healing of the survivor of ritual sex abuse is the same as for other abuses, but there are some extremely important additional precautions and needs. The therapist who deals with this situation needs to be very knowledgeable of this whole area and the aftermath of ritual sex abuse. Therapists who deal with such survivors need their own support group and consultation amongst each other because of the emotional drain and dangers that are associated with treating such people.

A therapist should operate under the assumption that a multiple personality disorder is present. One or more of the personalities may still be controlled by the cult, may be perpetrators themselves, and may try to sabotage therapy. They can also become threatening or dangerous.

The first stages of therapy should center on trust and safety. The ritual cult survivor has been reportedly deceived,

---

*Colin A. Ross, M.D., F.R.C.P. (C), et al., "Structured Interview Data on 102 Cases of Multiple Personality Disorder from Four Centers," *American Journal of Psychiatry* 147:5 (May 1990) 596–601.

**Carol Nadelson, M.D., and Derek Polonsky, M.D., "Childhood Sexual Abuse: The Invisible Ghost in Couple Therapy," *Psychiatric Annals* 21:8 (August 1991) 479–84.

manipulated, and tortured. The beginning process for healing then requires for the therapist to be non-threatening. This is accomplished by very carefully explaining the therapeutic process, clinic and office procedures, limits, and the concept of therapeutic contracts. Issues about confidentiality need to be explained and the conditions in which confidentiality would be broken. The survivor should be told that disturbing and destructive memories will be coming out at some point, and this is necessary for healing, but care will be taken to keep them from getting out of control.

A strong therapeutic alliance is crucial for the healing process to take place. Because the survivor has memories and fragments of memories that are horrible and overwhelming, the therapist must proceed cautiously and slowly and be ready to back off if the survivor is becoming overly stressed or disorganized. Many therapists find it helpful to teach the survivor to think of and visualize a safe, secure place to which he or she can retreat and get away from the destructive memories when there is the risk of being overwhelmed by them.

Safety Considerations

Safety for the survivor can include such things as avoiding known cultic places and people, and sharing mail and answering-machine messages with the therapist (to counter possible trigger messages that would place the survivor under a pre-programmed behavior.) The survivor can be told that confidentiality will be honored unless there is a threat to the therapist or family. In that case, there will be information in a lock box that will be turned over to appropriate authorities. This serves notice to the alternate personalities of an individual suffering from multiple personality disorder and thus secondarily to cultic members who may have access to these alters. They will realize they risk exposure if they become actively aggressive. This may protect both therapist and survivor from attack. One of the therapists in our clinic made this very explicit after receiving a very threatening letter written in blood.

It is also important to avoid adversarial positions, particularly in early stages of therapy. Such positions as Christianity versus Satanism, or you and the survivor versus the cult, can produce some unexpected problems. After all, part of the survivor may be so identified with the cult and its destructive practices that an adversarial position taken by the therapist is an attack on part of the survivor. The survivor and any listening alters need to hear that it is the therapist's belief that the person has experienced pain, confusion, and fear. This has resulted in alters who have reacted in various ways—some helpful, some not helpful. Each has something positive to contribute if there is healing from the traumatic experience so that the alters can cooperate and integrate with each other into a more complete, satisfying whole. This will be a joint venture between alters and therapist.

The Time for Education

At a point when the therapeutic alliance is secure and the survivor is reasonably comfortable with the therapist, he or she needs education about cults, their goals, and how they work. It is important to take away the sense of doom and magical power that has been implanted in these victims. They need to know the truth about Christianity, the significance of love, grace, and forgiveness. Their own areas of guilt should not be dismissed lightly just because they were under the control of other people. They do need to understand that they still need to be able to express in depth their own sense of guilt from involvement in ritualistic activities and possible terrible things they have done. When they have plumbed the depths of this submerged experience, they need to know there is no act, no matter how horrible, that cannot be totally forgiven and healed through Jesus Christ.

Pressure should not be placed on the survivor to forgive the perpetrators in the early stages of treatment. These people need to be able to plumb the almost bottomless pit of the extent of their fear, rage, helplessness, and hopelessness. Premature interventions to "turn it all over to the Lord" can block the healing process. There does come a point, however, later in therapy, when it will be important for persons who have been abused to release perpetrators and events to the Lord, but not get sidetracked or feel guilty over whether they have forgiven them or not. A more constructive step in that regard is to have survivors be willing to release the other people to the Lord for His intervention and to release their own anger so that they will not continue to be poisoned by the perpetrators. If they simply position themselves under the lordship of Jesus Christ and are willing to let Him deal with whether they can develop a sense of forgiveness in His hands, they need not get stuck on that issue.

The Importance of Support from an Enlightened Christian Group

These people need a new, powerful, loving, supportive group to promote further healing and correction from having been involved in a horribly destructive group sometimes for many years. This is where an enlightened subgroup of the body of Christ could be extremely helpful if they know something about this condition and do not short-circuit the therapeutic process with clichés and instant cure concepts. While unenlightened Christian groups have often caused damage by casting out nonexistent demons and giving advice as if some quick cure could come with the right attitude or the right prayer, it should still be emphasized that all of us, and particularly these folk, are engaged in spiritual warfare, and the ultimate victory does come through the grace and power of Jesus Christ. What is needed is a slow and thorough explanation of all the facets of the abuse and their reactions to it, engagement of the multiple personalities with the ultimate goal of gaining their cooperation, and finally integration into the total person. Prayer and the acceptance of God's grace, love, and forgiveness should not be used to sidetrack or interrupt this process, but rather seen as the ultimate power and healing that can bring extra hope and wholeness as the various facets of the therapeutic process come to light and, when the timing is right, are released to the Lord.

WORKBOOK

(Two pages are reserved here for your use in making notes on the foregoing discussion.)

3.

In Darkness and Pain—
Personal Stories of the
Effects of Sexual Abuse

For the enemy has persecuted my soul;
He has crushed my life to the ground;
He has made me dwell in dark places, like those
who have long been dead.
— Psalm 143:3, NASB

This chapter may well be one of the most important in the book for you. In it you will find brief comments from a number of victims of sexual abuse, each a different expression of the effects of different kinds of abuse. In some of these responses you may recognize ways in which you too have reacted to sexual abuse in your life and thus be able to begin dealing with the emotional and behavioral impact those experiences have had upon you.

As you listen to the stories shared here, pay particular attention to the disclosures of the day-to-day problems that have confronted these individuals in their struggle to overcome the darkness caused by sexual abuse. Through the problems of another individual it may be easier to place your own difficulties into more realistic perspective.

Pam, a tall, slender young woman who came to Rapha Treatment Centers for counseling, was given a book on sexual abuse with a list of characteristics of sexually abused victims. As she reviewed the list, she slumped into a chair and began to cry. For the first time her life made sense. Although Pam couldn't remember most of her childhood, she was carrying a big load of pent-up rage inside, along with much guilt and shame. But now, after looking at her situation in a new way, she was able to see herself as normal, or at least normal for what had happened to her as a child.

Headaches

"My headaches started very early. People would say to me, 'Marcy, you're too young to have headaches.' The headaches stopped for awhile, but now they last for days and often I am sick at my stomach. I don't even try to go to a doctor or even pray anymore. But God, how I wish they would stop."

Redness/Itching/Pain

"I kept taking my six-year-old to the pediatrician with yeast infections. I would tell him how red she was in the vaginal area. He would tell me it was from the milk she drank or antibiotics she'd taken. But one day my daughter told me about her uncle."

Sleeplessness

"I am nineteen and healthy, but a sleepaholic. Everyone teases me because I can sleep in any position, or at any time. What they don't know is that every night is torture. I can't go to sleep. I hate the night. I will clean anything just to stay awake. I will watch anything on TV to stay awake. I hear every noise. I am always so tired, but most of all I am so afraid."

Promiscuity

"I am thirty-two years old, have been married two times, and now am single again. There is so very much I long to do in my life, but what I want most is to be able to tell people I am not going to have sex with them. I can't seem to stop. Right now, I am sleeping with four people. I hate myself. One came by the other night and I didn't answer the door. Oh, God! I hope this means I am getting better!"

Rage and Depression

"I realize now that I have been depressed most of my life, at least from the time the abuse started. The first thing I remember is that I can't believe this is happening to me. Then I felt very angry. I wanted to hit things and I did. I would take the neighbor's cat and throw him out the window upside down, but he would always end up on his feet and walk away. I hated that cat for living. I hated myself for living. I felt so guilty. I knew it must be my fault. I still feel sad inside, I still don't want to do anything—anything, that is, but lie down."

Rage and Hatred

"People have told me I act like I have a terrible rage within, and you know what, it's just like that for me. I look at my children and I see the fear in their eyes. It breaks my heart. I never wanted to yell and scream like I did. Like I do. I hate myself for it. Sometimes I think I'm just too full of this hate. It just pours out of me at everyone. My husband can tell you about it. My family can tell you about it. The lady in the store can tell you about it. I can't control it."

Low Self-Esteem

"No, I don't feel good about myself. How could I? I was told again and again that I was no good. It was never what I wanted, it was only what he wanted. I didn't matter. But then, why should I? I really am nothing. I can't keep my mind on anything. I'm not smart like other people. Most of the time I don't even know where I really am. I do know this, though—

I wish I could be somebody else. I feel so worthless. My step-dad wasn't the only one, so I guess the rest were my fault. They said it was. They said it was, like, the way I looked, and that I really wanted them. I do hate myself. There's not much good about me. When I look into the mirror, all I see is this fat, ugly person."

Inability to Say No

"I guess it would be funny if it wasn't so sad. I can't say no to anyone. I can't say no if they want me to keep their kids. I can't say no if they ask, 'Do you have time to do this for me?' In fact, the only way I can say no is, 'No, of course I don't mind; I'll be happy to do this for you.' I am angry at myself when I don't say no, but I am afraid people won't like me if I don't say yes. I really feel helpless about it. I don't ever say no to anything. I feel angry, but most of all, I feel all used up."

Fear-Driven Reactions

"I was fifteen years old and we had moved across the country again. It was about 5 a.m. when we came into Los Angeles. We had stopped for breakfast. I needed to use the restroom, but once I was inside, I panicked when I heard someone about to come in the door. I fell onto the door like a madwoman, pushing as hard as I could. After a few seconds, a stout middle-aged female pushed the door open and stood glaring at me. I had completely humiliated myself. What had happened to me? I looked back at the woman and tried to smile at her. How could I explain to her what I couldn't explain to myself?"

Loss of Identity

"I was only seven years old when I told my therapist I thought I was gay. She asked me, 'What does gay mean?' I said it was bad, and I mumbled that it was when men had sex with each other. I felt so much anger and so much confusion I would crawl behind the couch in her office. She told me then that I might have these doubts about myself because of what had happened. She told me always be ready to come for help, but how do I know who I am? Am I male or female? Some people say being gay is normal, but it never felt good. I only wanted to see the snake the man had. It's like I got lost, my identity got lost. Who am I really?"

Double Messages

"I know I confuse my husband, how could I not? One moment I am all affectionate and romantic; I even want flowers and candlelight. But in a flash, I can completely change. I know a little now about working through my abuse. Was it a smell? Yes, oh my God! Yes, it was the onion on his breath. I prayed for rain every day, because then my daddy picked me up from school. If I walked home from school, there he was. He was so big and so mean! I really don't want to be one person one minute and another person another minute. How confusing for my husband, and my children. I just need to be alone now, if maybe I could just go away from everyone for awhile . . ."

He-Man Complex

"I brought my son Jason to the therapist because the school counselor said he had behavioral problems. I thought it was because my live-in boyfriend had whipped him real hard. Jason only wanted these 'he-man' toys. His favorites were always mean figures with guns or knives. I took him to the counselor for about seven months and he got better. She thought possibly he had been molested, but he always said no. I believed him until one day his step-sister told us about Steve's house. We all knew about Steve, because he had been arrested and sent to jail. People called him a pedophile. After a while in counseling my son didn't like those mean toys quite as much. All his drawings changed. They weren't monsters, giants and dragons. They weren't hideous anymore."

Codependency

"I read this book and it was true, I had no objectivity. I was either controlling or being controlled. It's like, *How can I figure it out? Why is this happening to me? My mother must know what's going on. I'm sure this isn't happening to anyone else.* But what gets me is that I never had a choice. Lots of parents drank, but my dad was so angry and my mom was so quiet. In fact, my mom was a mouse. She is still a mouse. The book was me, okay—I did everything it said. I was a legalist, in fact. If you were to be there at 3 p.m., you better be there! It's like that gave me some false sense of being in control of my life."

Self-Destructive Behavior

"I guess I did it all. By the age of thirteen I was sleeping with every guy who even *thought* he wanted it. So guess what—my mother sent me to my grandfather, and he loved having a great time with me. Maybe I hated him the most. Because every Sunday I had to listen to him preach. Of course, sex left me with nothing but a bad reputation. The alcohol helped me forget for a night, a day, but the effects never lasted. They say I am an alcoholic, but I don't drink anymore. I just eat and eat and eat. No one wants to have sex with me anymore. I'm glad. I still hate myself, but I do feel safe."

(*Note:* Some persons reflect self-hate and painful emotions by cutting and burning themselves. Others may engage in dangerous behavior such as shoplifting or driving recklessly.)

Memory Block

"I used to get so angry when people would talk about their childhood. Where was mine?! There aren't even any pictures! I only remember seeing my mother once, when I was six. I remember when my father, if you want to call him that, grabbed my hand and shoved it in my vagina and then shoved it in my face. I remember when I got the abortion. Nothing else. It's all gone! Where did it go? When I try to think back, I only remember a dark house and a dark room. It must have been my room. I can't remember holidays, Thanksgivings or even Christmases. Was it so bad that I checked out just so I could survive?"

Perfectionism

"I guess I am overly critical. I really criticize everything, but most of all my husband. Maybe my children would say I criticize them the most. I must have everything perfect. I just can't seem to let go. Okay doesn't seem good enough. It's true I want people to give *me* a break, and really, I want to give *them* a break. I just don't know how. I'm not as picky as people think. I just want everyone and everything to be in order.

" My husband is always saying, 'Can't you just give up this harping on always having everything perfect?' I wish I could. Really, I wish I knew how. I used to say 'that doesn't matter' and 'this doesn't matter.' Pretty soon, nothing mattered. That can't be right! I know I'm supposed to encourage my family, but when I do, it just comes out wrong. Sometimes I think maybe I am helping them to improve, to be a little more than they are."

Betrayal

"Well, all I can say is, if you have been abused, you have been betrayed. Everyone has betrayed you. Your mother, your father, and, most of all, God. My mom and dad watched me pretty good, but they put me with that babysitter. She was so mean and she would call me all sorts of names. She would sit me on her lap and make me pee between her legs. I hate her. They all betrayed me. But why am I so angry now? I believe everyone betrays me, even when they don't. My son forgets to turn out the light in the kitchen and I lose my cool. It's like he purposely didn't turn the light out, just to hurt me. I know it's crazy, because he is really just a kid who forgets to turn the light out. I test everybody to see if they will betray me. I guess I'm trying to get what I never had. It's a need that someone would really be there for me."

Fear

"I fear being alone. I fear being abandoned. I fear going to sleep. I fear almost everything. Once I couldn't take a job because it was across town. I could drive around the town, but if I went through town, I feared I couldn't get back home. I fear that everyone knows who I really am. I fear the thoughts I have.

"My mind is full of all the bad things that might happen. When I was ten, I would ask myself, *What if the house burns down?* or, *What happens if I can't get to school?* I am afraid of having friends and of even going to church. I fear that people won't approve of me and that they will reject me. I am so afraid most of the time that I don't try things, because I'm afraid I would fail or get hurt, but most of all I am afraid I won't get better."

Withdrawal

"Of all the things I have ever done in life, the thing I do best is withdraw. I have even been to parties and stayed in the bathroom for as long as I could without embarrassing myself even more. At seventeen I got my first job. I would take my break in the bathroom. Really, I don't have a thing for bathrooms. I have all sorts of ways to isolate myself. I stay too busy and am constantly announcing to people that I don't have any time. If I've mastered anything, it's the ability to tell you nothing about myself except that I am fine. I even withdraw from my family by having headaches and going to my room. Sometimes even when I don't want to feel anything, I get a little scared because I do feel all alone."

Anxiety/Sense of Doom

"Sometimes when I'm sitting in class and everyone has left the room, I feel something evil. I will turn around to see if anyone is there. When I go into my bedroom, it's the same feeling. It sounds so silly, but I check under the bed, and I check in my closet. I can't stand it when the shower curtain is closed. I get real anxious for no reason—or it seems to me for no reason. I sometimes feel if I move, I'll bump into something—something bad. I stay real still and try to concentrate real hard. Sometimes I ask for Jesus to help me. I really hate this feeling."

Repeated Victimization

"I think the first one who abused me was my step-dad. As far as I can remember, he touched me in my vagina. I think it only happened once. Then, a couple of years later, when my mom and I were living alone, it happened again. This time it was a pervert who would stand in the window of his apartment completely nude with a large erection. He would stand there glaring at me when I came home from school. Next I was abused by an uncle and then later by my brother's friends.

"I thought it would all end when I got married, but it *really* started then. My husband drank like a fish and demanded sex all the time, and 'anything would go.' One day he said he was bored with me and he left. There was a boyfriend, then another husband. Nothing ever seemed to change in my life. I got knocked around a couple of times, but the bomb dropped when I got raped."

Seductive Behavior

"All my life they said I dressed sexy. I didn't know what they were talking about. I just dressed like everyone else. They said I was 'boy-crazy.' And they were right about that— I had lots of boyfriends. But they said I attracted all the wrong guys.

"I was determined to stay a virgin until I got married. It was real hard and a few times I almost didn't make it. I had been masturbating since I was about five. I got in a lot of trouble whenever my mom would catch me. So, I just got more careful. Anyway, I think this helped me to wait until I got married.

"I got married, but then I began to hate sex. I couldn't believe it! It would hurt so bad, but the doctor said there was nothing wrong with me. He said it was 'in my mind.' Then I got divorced, and I began to sleep with one guy after another. I counted them once, and it was twenty. Sex didn't hurt anymore, but it never felt good either."

You have just read what 22 individuals have had to say about the effects of sexual abuse in their lives. We have deliberately not included any examples having to do with altered states of consciousness (blackouts, depersonalization, multiple personality disorder, etc.), which are often found among sexual abuse victims. Individuals who suffer from any of these altered states require treatment from trained specialists, as noted in the previous chapter.

Some victims suddenly black out as they may have done when they were being abused. Whatever you have discovered and been able to associate with the abuse in your life is a powerful start to recovery. To identify the effects helps in putting things in perspective in your life. Identifying effects provides a framework to develop specific goals for recovery and directions for your prayers.

Please complete the workbook questions at the end of this chapter. And don't be afraid to take one more step in recovery. Read the list of "Overcomer's Hopes" on the following page. It is there to give you encouragement because looking at the effects of sexual abuse in your life may have overwhelmed you temporarily. As you read these hopes, understand that they are also God's promises—promises that He can bring to pass. At times you will get discouraged in your recovery process; when you do, take several moments to read these promises that God has for you. You may want to prepare your own personal list of hopes. People do recover from sexual abuse.

The Overcomer's Hopes

In Christ I can:
1. (1) live a life without fear controlling me.
2. (2) live a life without being controlled by others.
3. (3) live a life without condemnation or condemning others.
4. (4) live a life without shame and guilt.
5. (5) live a life where I know the difference between what is safe and what is not safe.
6. (6) live a life without rage, hate, and depression.
7. (7) live a life with stable emotions.
8. (8) live a life with joy and happiness—even in the midst of trials.
9. (9) live a life with peace and love.
10. (10) live a life without helplessness.
11. (11) live a life with appropriate sexual behavior.
12. (12) live a life understanding my value in Christ.
13. (13) live a life where I can be intimate with others.
14. (14) live a life where I can trust others who are trustworthy.
15. (15) live a life where I have a deep relationship with God.

WORKBOOK

1. From the stories told in this chapter pick at least one that you related to or identified with and describe your feelings about it.

2. How do you get away from the pain of your abuse? Do you isolate yourself or withdraw from people and experiences? Give one example.

3. Draw a picture of significant people in your life now or in the past.

4. From your childhood experiences, describe your feelings and the circumstances when you felt most powerful, most afraid, most angry, and most sad.

5. Read the scripture quoted just below the title of this chapter on page 27, and then tell what it says to you.

6. Describe your self-image. List at least three strengths and weaknesses that are a direct result of sexual abuse. How do you see yourself? Draw a picture of your strong self and a picture of your weak self. Talk about them.

7. Describe the impact that sexual abuse has had on your vocational relationships.

8. Describe the effects of sexual abuse upon your personal relationships (family, spouse, children).

9. If you have repeatedly been victimized in your life, describe those experiences and your reactions.

10. How have you dealt with unmet needs resulting from your being a victim?

4.

The Family in Darkness—
Relationships and Responsibility

For this reason I kneel before the Father, from whom his whole family in heaven and on earth derives its name. I pray that . . . he may strengthen you with power through his Spirit in your inner being.

—Ephesians 3:14–16, NIV

Family issues have a tremendous effect on sexual abuse recovery. A family shaken by the tragedy of such abuse is a family in a shroud of darkness. Some parents and other family members may have been perpetrators, while others were oblivious to the fact abuse occurred. Whatever your case may be, with the help of God you can understand the role your family played in your sexual abuse.

Victims of incest in which the father is the perpetrator must also deal with anger toward the mother. A child molested by an uncle may feel unprotected by both parents. A victim of rape may feel she cannot disclose that fact to her family because her family is emotionally shut down and incapable of giving her support. In families where the child is abused by a baby-sitter, the child, as we would expect, has been told to obey the sitter. Often this victim has a great deal of anger toward both parents; the child believes the parents must know what is going on.

Too Busy to Listen

Gretchen describes many bizarre incidents of her abuse by her baby-sitter. Sometimes she had to watch the sitter and her boyfriend have sex. Sometimes the baby-sitter would fondle her or would stick straws, pencils, and other such objects into her vagina or anus. She would tell Gretchen that she was bad and that she was ugly. Gretchen hated the baby-sitter and hated her parents. Although she tried many times to tell her mom and dad about the abuse, they were so busy with their own problems that they didn't seem to care or even pay attention to her. Her father was out of work and her mother was pregnant. They scolded her for making a fuss about nothing.

Finally Gretchen told her parents loudly and clearly. In fact, she screamed and yelled the whole gruesome story. Both parents were shocked. They couldn't believe it. Gretchen had really been irritable, but they never dreamed what was going on while they were gone.

Although Gretchen's parents actually were supportive of her in general, the abuse had come at a very troubled time of preoccupation for the family. Once aware, however, the parents brought Gretchen to counseling and participated in family counseling as well as individual counseling. In counseling, Gretchen expressed her appropriate anger toward her parents. The parents accepted the responsibility for their seeming lack of interest, selection of the baby-sitter, and failure to recognize Gretchen's attempts to communicate..

Dysfunctional Families

Gretchen's family was a fairly functional family, but in most of the families where sexual abuse occurs, the families are decidedly dysfunctional. The term *dysfunctional* is used here to express the inability of the family members to meet the God-given needs for nurturing in a family system. These families are unable to communicate in a consistent, loving way and rarely are functionally there to meet the needs of each family member.

Recovery on Her Own

Another example of a family in darkness is that of a young woman named Jean. The oldest of six children, Jean is very anxious and an alcoholic. Her father started abusing her at an early age. By the time she was ten, they were having intercourse. She consistently made protests to her mother, but her mother only replied, "What can I do?" Jean's mother was jealous of her daughter and her husband. As Jean began to recognize her mother's jealousy, she used it against both parents. By age sixteen, she couldn't stand the situation any longer and ran away and never returned.

Jean's mother still resents her and really doesn't try to have a relationship with her, her husband, or her child. Jean's father, on the other hand, wants everything to be okay. He wants Jean just to forget the past. Jean is in the process of working out her own recovery. Although it would be extremely helpful if her family would also enter the recovery program, Jean is beginning to realize that her dysfunctional mother and father are unwilling to do so at this time. She is accepting the fact that she must continue in recovery on her own and no longer look for them to change so that she can feel all right.

A Pattern of Avoiding Embarrassment

Still another family example is one that looked perfectly normal on the surface. The father and mother did most of the things that parents should do. They kept an orderly house, a nice yard, food on the table, and clothes in the closet. However, this mother and father were not emotionally present for their children. One child, Beatrice, was a volunteer for the local rape crisis center. She became a victim herself, after being raped at knifepoint.

The rape occurred one morning when Beatrice, after being

with a few friends for breakfast, returned to her apartment. Hearing a knock at the door, she peeked out and saw a man she knew, although not very well. She asked what he wanted. "I need to talk to someone," he said. One rule that typical crisis centers teach is never to open the door under such circumstances. Unfortunately, Beatrice did open the door and was raped. She received serious wounds, but decided she didn't want to press charges.

I asked her why she, of all people, didn't do so. She replied that her parents told her it was her fault for opening the door and if she were to follow through on the charges, it would only cause embarrassment for the family. She said it was just like when she tried to tell them about her grandfather. She was black and blue all over from the beating he gave her. All her parents could say was, "He didn't mean what he did," and, "What did you do to cause it?"

With her family's pattern of telling her to keep everything quiet, Beatrice must go through recovery without family support.

A Biblical Story of Family Dysfunction

The Bible records a similar story in chapter 13 of 2 Samuel. Amnon, one of King David's sons, was lovesick for his half-sister, Tamar. He feigned an illness in order to lure Tamar into his chamber: "He took hold of her and said to her, 'Come, lie with me, my sister.' But she answered him, 'No, my brother, do not violate me, for such a thing is not done in Israel: do not do this disgraceful thing.' . . . However, he would not listen to her."

Tamar reported the incident to one of her other brothers, Absalom. The story continues: "Then Absalom her brother said to her . . . 'but now keep silent, my sister, he is your brother; do not take this matter to heart.' So Tamar remained and was desolate in her brother Absalom's house" (2 Sam. 13:11–12, 14, 20).

It seems that the pattern was no different for a dysfunctional family in biblical times than for a family in the present, like Beatrice's. The problem for victims is also the same—when they remain silent, they become desolate. Discussing your abuse does not mean getting up in church and announcing to everyone that you have been sexually abused, but it does mean for you, as a victim, to tell the story in a safe, supportive environment, and to tell it until God has healed the pain. Dysfunctional persons, many times, have to learn what a safe place is.

When Samuel said that Tamar remained in her brother's house and was desolate, he was saying that she was forlorn and lonely, without friends or hope. Over and over again the victim is left without deep friendships and without hope. Often the victim is forced into isolation, left alone, and in great despair.

The Vulnerable Single-Parent Family

Another kind of family that is vulnerable to abuse is the single-parent family where the mother is the head of the household. Children in this family may be with a babysitter, left alone, or in the presence of strangers more often than other children. Such circumstances can increase the chances for a child to be victimized.

Ten-year-old Naomi describes how excited she was when a certain man first started dating her mom. Her mom was so happy and smiled all the time. "I just couldn't tell her when he started touching me," Naomi said. "I began to think maybe he just wanted to marry her because of me. They got married. I hated that day. Eventually he made me have sex with him again and again. He was so big and fat and sweaty. I really hate him.

"When it finally came out, my mom was so sad. After a while he convinced her he was sorry. He began to treat her real nice. She was like she was on her honeymoon again.

Charges were never pressed against him, and everybody was so happy except me." Sexually abused children from these single-parent families deal with not only the sexual abuse, but with the loneliness and pain caused by the divorce and the lessened contact with the parent they live with. I do not mean to be critical of a single-parent family system, but only to help the victim discover all the pieces that will aid his or her full recovery.

The Dysfunctional Family and Alcohol and Drug Abuse

Other families with increased potential for sexual abuse are those in which alcohol or drugs were abused. Some of you who are reading this book may have come from a family where you were the scapegoat even though no chemical abuse was present. Perhaps a role-reversal situation was established in the family system when you were at an early age. Children caught in role-reversal, where they must play adult to their parents' child figure, think that they are responsible for making everything all right, but they do not know how to do it. These children become the parents, and their parents become children.

"My mother was so sweet and loving. When Dad died my mom started saying, 'Charlie, my little man. My Charlie is the man of this house.' I was so scared by that, I didn't know what I was supposed to do. I couldn't make much money; I was too young. When the man who hurt me came into our lives, he said he would teach me to be a man. He said I would like being a man. I did, because men could be angry. I wanted all my toys to be war or defense toys. I learned karate and became very good at it.

"The horrible part for me was to admit I was a victim. Men are not victims, that's woman stuff. I was tough. How sad for me—I never got to be just a little boy. My dad died when I was five and that man moved in with my mother and me when I was ten."

The Authoritative Family System

Another example of a family at risk is the one with an authoritative family system. This family is usually dominated by the father who has a submissive wife. Brooke describes how she felt about her family and her abuse. "I guess the reason I hated God so much is because my father quoted God so much. It seemed everything he did was right out of the Bible. He would always quote the scriptures to all of us, saying that he was the master. He never hit or paddled us or otherwise physically hurt us. We were all afraid of him. There were three of us girls and we all got sexually abused. Not one of us told Mother. She was already so sick, what difference did it make? It is really hard for me to believe in a loving God, especially when you call him Father."

The Movable "Home"

Victims of abuse may also have lived with more than one family, perhaps first with mother and father and next with grandmother and grandfather. In my childhood, I attended nineteen different schools, including five during my high school years. I lived with my mother, my grandmother, my mother and stepfathers, my sister's father, and with several other family systems. Each one presented different challenges for my recovery. I had to deal with emotional abuse, chaos, and the aftermath of my sexual abuse, all of which made me think that I was profoundly inadequate as a person, since I was unable to alter or control what was happening. The lesson I learned from all of this was that I could do nothing about my life. No matter what I tried to change, it didn't work. No matter what I did to bring order, chaos always resulted. And I could not make sense out of chaos.

I had to carry the outside shame of moving so many times along with the inside shame of the sexual abuse. When I left for school in the morning, I didn't know if things would be the same when I got home. I trusted no one because if outsiders knew my story, my pain was greater. I not only acted toward others as if I didn't care, I began to shut down so I wouldn't care. I would say to myself, "Only breathing matters, and I am breathing." But, of course, breathing by itself is not living. Also, several of the people responsible for my care were alcoholics, which added to my confusion and lowered my self-worth.

Each family system teaches us something very deep about ourselves, and not always positive. The sexual abuse and the chaos in my family taught me that I was profoundly inadequate. But there was also positive learning. My mother said again and again, "Don't do as I have done, I've done it all wrong. You can do it better." She taught me that I was smart; that I could do it. She taught me that there was a better way. She didn't know that better way, but she taught me that if I searched hard enough, I could find it. She was right. I found it with God.

Learning to Interpret the Messages

Each family member sends us messages about ourselves. The perpetrator of sexual abuse says, "You're worthless. You are no good and you are guilty." Maybe your father or mother sent you the same message, not by sexual abuse but by his or her words and attitudes. Maybe a sister told you you were stupid. Maybe you had a granddad who said you were special—a badly needed positive reinforcement. Consider the messages that each person and perpetrator gave you in your life.

Many families transmit messages that say, *Don't express your feelings; Don't cry, Don't get upset, Don't get angry; Don't betray the family, Don't ever tell outsiders about the family secrets.* These messages, as well as ones more directly stated toward you, affect your recovery. You may have been told that you are no good, that you are a failure, or shamed by any number of derogatory statements—all of these are characteristic of a family based in shame.

In his book *Search for Significance*,* Robert McGee discusses four common false beliefs perpetuated in part by dysfunctional families and almost certain to be held by the victim as truths. McGee emphasizes that these false beliefs will create guilt, a false sense of responsibility, low self-worth, and a host of other issues for the victim.

One of these beliefs is that *I must meet certain standards in order to feel good about myself.* Whatever standards we have set are in part based on the messages we heard as we were growing up. Believing the statement we have just articulated blocks us from realizing that we are already fully pleasing to God. No matter how intense, perfect, or successful we become, meeting falsely motivated standards will not bring us the peace we desire.

I must have others' approval is another of the false messages transmitted by families, says McGee. Conveyed over and over in our daily lives, it convinces us that we were not good enough and that no one could really love us. We become consumed with pleasing others at any cost. Accordingly, the fear of rejection or anyone's disapproval overwhelms us with fear.

Next on the list is *Because I have failed, I am unworthy and deserve to be punished.* If someone else doesn't punish us, we will punish ourselves. This sense of unworthiness must be recognized for what it is.

The final negative statement on McGee's list declares, *I am what I am; I cannot change; I am hopeless.* The family in darkness places the victim in an environment that teaches this hopelessness.

---

*Robert S. McGee, *The Search for Significance*, 2d ed. (Houston, TX: Rapha Publishing, 1990), p. 122.

Touching

By contrast, building a healthy self-image in a child, an adult, or in a recovering sexual abuse victim requires everyday reinforcement in terms that demonstrate that person's value, not only in positive statements but also in physical contact. The part played by touching has received considerable attention in recent years, especially in the importance of bonding between infant and mother and father. Unfortunately, sometimes in a family in darkness the only touching we may have experienced may have been bad touching. These touches may have been extremely confusing, as God created us to express affection. He created us to give and receive healthy physical love, such as hugging, holding hands, and kissing.

If the only touch in your family was the wrong touch, you were totally deprived of a natural family function. You may have even felt guilty because you so much wanted to be held but the only time you received this attention was during abuse. That was a double tragedy, but you can begin to see light in this darkness. You were not wrong for wanting and needing what God intended you to have in a healthy manner.

Fantasy Bonding

One further problem sometimes found in the family in darkness is fantasy bonding between certain family members. M. J. describes one such situation. "All my life I would think back and remember how my sister and I were best friends, how she was always there for me. I would remember how she cooked for me. How she dressed me in the mornings for school. How she loved me. What I couldn't figure out was that now that we were adults, she never came to see me. I was always the one who went to her house, and I always called her on the phone.

"It took a long time, but I finally realized it was all make-believe. This 'bonding' was a way I had learned to cope in my loneliness as a child. My mother had made her take care of me. I realize now that she didn't even want to. As we sat on the porch holding hands, I would fantasize that she loved me. This love, this relationship was only in my mind; it never really existed. The reason she never called now was because she didn't want to. She never came to my house because she didn't want to."

You may need to seek God's wisdom to become aware of fantasy bonding with any family members. I urge you to do so, for this knowledge can set you on the true path to having real relationships with these relatives. Even if they are not what you thought or even what you wanted, they will be authentic relationships that you can understand and predict. Your efforts may even lead to loving and intimate relationships, if your relatives are willing to consider honestly all the factors affecting your former situation.

Reaching Out for Help

Working through these family issues is painful and will probably continue to be so. If you feel desolate, betrayed, and alone, reach out to someone who can help you. You might join a sexual abuse overcomers' group, or begin individual counseling to break the feeling of shame over your abuse.

However you choose to pursue recovery, it is most important to receive the support God wants you to have to overcome this tragedy. It is His intention for you to walk in joy and peace, free from guilt and condemnation. I recommend seeking professional help during your recovery process.

Who Is My Family?

As you recover, you may be surprised to find that some family members may also pursue recovery from former behavior patterns. I started my recovery many years ago and as I have progressed through it, many of my own family members have also entered the process. Now I truly do have some functional and loving relationships with them.

Even so, I have learned to allow God to become my closest family. I didn't give up my family, but I have placed God at the center. He has become the family support, the family love, and the family unit I did not have.

As I have learned to do, you can allow God to replace your feelings of unworthiness with His facts about your worthiness. He can replace your hopelessness with hope in Christ and your profound feelings of inadequacy with adequacy found only in Him. Remember that you are deeply loved by Him, fully pleasing to Him, and totally accepted by Him. You are totally acceptable.

Whatever your family system, try to grasp the effect this system had on you. Pray to comprehend the predominant message each member sent you about yourself. Ask God to help you recognize any sinful ways you have used to compensate for your feelings of inadequacy. Explore any fantasy bonding between you and your family that is distracting you from your search for truth.

Messages of Support and Love

On the following page is a list of 22 messages God has given you through His Word. Take time to read the entire list of messages each day for 22 days. Read and meditate on a different one of the accompanying scriptures each day. Allow God to restore to you all that was taken by your family. Allow God to nurture you, comfort you, and encourage you. Trust God to love you even if no one else has ever loved you.

Scripture Reference	God's Messages to You as a Believer
Genesis 1:26–27	I am uniquely created in God's image.
Matthew 5:13	I am the salt of the earth.
Matthew 5:14	I am the light of the world.
Luke 11:9–10	I ask and receive; I seek and find; I knock and the door is opened unto me.
John 8:32	The truth has set me free.
John 14:27	I have peace.
John 17:18	I have been sent into the world.
John 17:22	I have God's glory.
Acts 13:38	I have forgiveness of sins through Christ.
Romans 8:1	I now have no condemnation.
Romans 8:32	I have all things.
Romans 12:6	I have been given gifts.
1 Corinthians 2:16	I have the mind of Christ.
1 Corinthians 3:9	I am God's fellow-worker; I am God's field, God's building.
2 Corinthians 4:16	My inner self is being renewed day by day.
Ephesians 3:20	I have a power source within me which is able to do exceeding abundantly beyond all that I ask or think.
Philippians 4:7	The peace of God guards my heart and mind.
Philippians 4:13	I can do all things through Him who strengthens me.
Philippians 4:19	God shall supply all my needs according to His riches in glory in Christ Jesus.
2 Timothy 1:7	For God has not given me a spirit of timidity, but of power and love and discipline.
Philemon 6	The knowledge of every good thing is in me.
1 Peter 2:9–10	I am chosen.

WORKBOOK

1. Describe your family, listing all the primary members. What does each individual represent to you? How do you feel about each individual?

2. Complete the word association quiz found on pp. 273–74, responding with the first thought that comes to mind. (If you are not able to give an immediate answer, move on to the next item; remember that no response is also a response.) What insight, if any, does this give you about your relationships with family members?

3. What predominant message did each family member give you about yourself? What did the messages make you feel about yourself?

4. How have you responded to or compensated for the good and the bad messages?

5. Read the story of Tamar in 2 Samuel 13:1–20 and describe how this makes you feel.

6. Apart from your sexual abuse, what issues do you need to process as a result of your relationships with your family and their treatment of you?

7. If you were abused by a family member, did your family perpetrator send you the same messages as other members of your family? If so, what were they? If not, how were they different? How do you feel about those messages?

8. Reread the four negative statements discussed by author Robert McGee on page 50. Did you receive any of these messages from your family as you were growing up? If so, how have they affected your feelings and relationships?

9. Describe in detail any fantasy bonding you may have with family members.

10. If your family chooses not to pursue recovery from dysfunctional behavior, how might this decision affect your recovery? Your future?

5.

Believing the Darkness—
Lies versus Truths

All joy is darkened;
the gaiety of the earth is banished.
—Isaiah 24:11, NASB

The experience of being sexually abused almost always leaves its victims with a very damaging set of false beliefs. Held as irrefutable truths, these erroneous ideas create mistaken guilt, destroy self-esteem, and assign undeserved responsibility for what has happened to individuals who have already suffered devastating emotional and physical trauma. Victims often pay lip service to the falsity of these beliefs and even seem to comprehend their effects in their lives. They will, however, still suffer the consequences of these damaging thoughts until they replace them with the truth in their inner beings.

Christians in addition often confuse what they know to be scriptural truth with the overwhelming emotions they experience. They long to believe all God tells them in His Word, yet they have difficulty bringing the truth into their hearts and living it out in their everyday lives.

Continuing to base their reactions to people and situations upon such false beliefs will lead sexually abused people to a life filled with anguish and pain. Victims will still look to family to fix their lives, especially if the perpetrator was a family member. Victims will try to have needs met by the dysfunctional family system.

Victims will often be unable to enjoy healthy sexual interaction with their spouses. The false beliefs of the victims often keep them full of fear and even revulsion toward sex. Some adult victims are even unable to express healthy affection with their children, while other victims try to have needs met through sexual interaction and become involved in sexual addiction and promiscuity.

Victims also try to cope with feelings of guilt and abuse. They will think of themselves as dirty or as undeserving of respect. Maintaining this false belief often sets victims up for being revictimized. Believing the false beliefs will keep them in depression. Sometimes victims become so hopeless that they must overcome the torment of suicidal thoughts.

The Abused Child's Tragic Loss

Children who have been sexually molested rarely have the emotional maturity to deal with what is happening to them. In most cases, their physical and mental maturation is not reached until at least their late teens. Once children have been violated, however, their normal maturation process has been severely damaged and may never be completed.

The situation with which sexually abused children must cope is difficult to comprehend even for adults suffering the same victimization. Children lose their rightful identities as loved and valuable human beings, and they must try to mature in a life whose foundation is based in confusion and betrayal. Many factors enter into the healthy development of children, but false beliefs that are established as they are growing up will become a significant part of their emotional instability as adults.

"It's My Fault!"

A common misconception for the child is that the abuse is his or her fault. Five-year-old Lisa was describing the horror of having semen in her mouth by making a distorted face and whining about the taste. "It was my fault," she told me during a counseling session.

"It was not your fault," I responded. "You are only five years old. Your father is the adult, and he was the one who decided to do this thing to you. In fact, as you've told me before, you didn't want to do it, but your father made you do it. Many times you've told me how much you hated it. Do you understand that it's your father's fault, and not your fault?"

"Oh, yes," she said, "I know it's my daddy's fault. He always told me it was both our fault. We would say what we were doing was my fault and his fault."

Lisa's understanding of the relationship between herself as child victim and her father is typical. The perpetrator establishes in the child's mind the concept of "we." "We" are doing this; therefore "we" are responsible. As the child matures, this concept of "we" becomes more and more firmly cemented in her or his mind because the child begins to think of all the times he or she could have asked the father to stop the abuse but didn't. The reality, of course, is that the child rarely, if ever, could have gotten the abuse stopped.

When children are told that what has happened is their fault, they accept total responsibility for the abuse. Even adult women who have been raped deal with this issue. Rape victims will say such things as "If I hadn't been here, or there," "If I hadn't answered the door," etc. Often rapists will yell filthy accusations at their victims as the rape is in progress. During this time of great fear and despair, these adult victims will begin to believe the lies.

Obviously, children have even less ability to comprehend the truth of the situation. As they try to process what is happening to them, they will wrongly accept the responsibility. Even after years of having helped many children, I am still dismayed that following a lapse of only a few sessions, during which I thought I had firmly established in their minds that the abuse was the perpetrator's full responsibility, so many of them would return to me saying no, it was their fault. I have found this false belief so firmly fixed in the minds of young victims that I now routinely begin each session stressing the fact that the abuse was not the child's fault.

"Grown-ups Can't Do Wrong!"

Most children want to believe, or in fact *do* believe, that adults can do no wrong. They view parents as almost God-like. To children, adults are all-powerful and all-knowing, and it is hard for them to accept the idea that an adult would do something wrong. Generally, when they do think of an adult as having done something bad, they still feel as if they made the adult do it. Children of abuse think that this "bad thing" which is happening to them must be their own fault: *I must be a really terrible little girl for my daddy to do this*, and just so with hundreds of such interpretations.

An equally common false belief is *I wanted him (or her) to do this to me*. Natalie, a ten-year-old, explained that she must have wanted her stepdaddy to fondle her because she loved sitting on his lap. She really loved her real daddy, but he had to work long hours and couldn't come see her. Her new dad made her feel special and gave her lots of attention. "He told me he was going to make me feel real good and I would really like what he was going to do. It did tickle and I did feel real, real close to him. I guess I liked it. But after a while, it wasn't much fun.

"He made me feel so grown up," she continued. "He gave me beer to drink and I would twirl around. Sometimes what he was doing to me would hurt and then we would drink more beer. One day it really hurt. He said it would really hurt, but then he said it would feel good after awhile. And it did feel good. I must have gotten so I really wanted it, just like he said, because when everybody found out and we stopped, I would rub and rub and rub myself so I could feel like that again."

Eleven-year-old Kevin described his uncle to me as someone who was always taking him places. He also said that his aunt and uncle fought all the time, but that was just their way. One day his uncle said to him, "I know how to make you feel real good. You're getting interested in girls, and I can show you how they can make you feel real good."

"Sure," Kevin agreed. He told me that, just like his uncle said, what happened did feel good. "But I knew it was wrong and I never wanted to do it again. But whenever we went anywhere, he always did it. I always let him, and the worst part is that it always felt good."

Normal Physiological Responses

Both the stories you have just read not only illustrate children's faith in what grownups tell them, but they also describe normal physiological responses in the human body that God has created. It is not unusual that these two children and thousands of other victims sometimes enjoyed some part of the stimulation that occurred during their molestation. Often, victims will speak with total disgust toward themselves because they have had a healthy physiological reaction to an unhealthy and illegal act perpetrated upon them.

It is not false to believe that the human body is created for healthy sexual interaction between husband and wife. It is a false belief to assume that you are a terrible individual because you had a normal physiological reaction to stimulation. It is just such a false belief that traps the victim's mind and holds it captive.

The Tragedy of Lost Self-Worth

The most common and probably the most devastating false beliefs are those that result in a feeling of low self-worth. Any statements we or others make that describe us in negative terms fall into this category—things like labeling ourselves "no good," "a failure," "stupid," "ugly," and the like. The tragedy is that, repeated often enough, we come to believe these falsehoods and eventually to act them out. In other words, if I consistently see myself as worthless, I will not be able to act worthwhile. Perhaps for a day or a week I can, but in time I will give up the pretense altogether.

Trish suffered a breakdown in self-worth through labels pasted onto her by her boyfriend. Now she tries to understand why she even has to go to school. "He told me I was worthless and no good when I turned him in. He said he picked me up from a trash pile. I guess that meant I was trash. Every day he said I was stupid, and my mother was stupid too because she never said anything or did anything. He said I was just like her and she was stupid. And you know what? She *was* stupid!—stupid not to love her own kid. She said she wasn't gonna say anything about him in court, and she didn't. I couldn't live with my mom anymore, and the kids at school always looked at me as if there was something wrong with me when they found out I didn't live with her. When I get to be fourteen, I'm not going to go to school, 'cause it doesn't matter. I don't matter."

There are many ways perpetrators' actions instill false beliefs in the lives of their victims. Perpetrators are usually "me first" individuals, and consequently what they want prevails. Most victims begin to believe that they have no real value. What is valued is what the perpetrators desire to take from the victims. The abuse teaches the victims that there are no boundaries. This is particularly harmful to children, who are not yet mature enough to understand boundaries and thus are often set up to be revictimized. Repeated victimization firmly fixes the idea of worthlessness in the victims' minds, regardless of age. They must truly be worthless or the abuse would not continue to happen. They are no good. People are no good.

When the Perpetrator Is a Significant Other

Most victims are violated by someone they know, most commonly a significant other, such as a father or stepfather. Children may make an attempt to disclose the abuse to a mother or significant other. Often children assume that a parents know what is happening, since they so often view parents as Godlike. They may ask, "Do you know what Daddy is doing to me?" or, "Do I have to do everything Suzie says?" Unfortunately, the parent or significant other may not always recognize children's attempts to disclose.

Parents, particularly, are not likely to believe that a spouse is engaging in such destructive behavior. Therefore, their need to deny the abuse can make recognition of the problem even greater. To further complicate the situation, children often attempt to disclose bad things that are happening to them through their behavior rather than simply by telling someone about it. They may display sexual behavior inappropriate for their age, or they may suddenly become unruly. Grades may begin to drop at school. They may engage in stealing or in some form of self-abuse. All of these behaviors can be methods of attempting to show that something is wrong. If no one picks up on their attempted disclosures, whether verbal or behavioral, children begin to feel that no one cares what is happening, and if no one cares, the idea that they must truly be worthless is reinforced.

The Importance of Validation

When victims verbally attempt to disclose, or do disclose, the reality of sexual abuse, it is very important that they be validated in what they have said. Most of the time, children will share only a portion of what they have experienced. Sometimes children will recant what they have disclosed if they sense anger and/or a nonsupportive attitude from the person(s) they have chosen to entrust. In most cases, children have not lied; they are only trying to avoid trouble.

If the victims of abuse are taken seriously and the abuse is stopped, their worth can be validated. A policeman with the Houston Police Department who works with women who have been raped says that, immediately after the rape, often women victims want male officers to help them through the initial period of fear and despair. Later, they usually desire a female officer, to whom they describe the terrible events that they have just been through. It is important for the officers, both male and female, to support the victim at each stage of need.

Understanding the Origin of False Beliefs

Many causes can be found for the false beliefs that commonly develop in those who have been sexually abused. The abuse itself, the perpetrators, the co-perpetrators, and various other considerations, such as the number of perpetrators involved, all play a role in promoting very destructive false beliefs about one's self-worth. It is crucial for victims to understand the origin of their false beliefs and to begin correcting them so that their self-perpetuating, destructive effects do not continue.

Many children, teenagers, and adults look into the mirror and tell themselves they are fat. They tell themselves they are ugly and that they hate their bodies. Many times these individuals are thin, attractive people.

A ten-year-old describes her dilemma. She is a beautiful blonde-headed child who is slightly underweight. "I can't figure out why I'm so fat, because some days I don't eat at all. Every time I look in the mirror, I think I am so ugly. I can even have a new dress and get my hair fixed, but when I look into the mirror all I see is this fat, ugly person. I always notice what's wrong with me. I know something is wrong with me, or it wouldn't have happened to me. Even God really hates me. I know it wasn't me that wanted to have the sex, so it must have been my body and that's why it happened. I hate me, I hate my body, and I hate everybody."

For recovery, victims must discover what false beliefs they hold and then rid themselves of them, permanently. *Telling Yourself the Truth*, a book by William Backus and Marie Chapian,* discusses the necessity of telling yourself the "real" truth. If whatever you are thinking about yourself has been distorted by abuse, they emphasize, you must solidly determine not to agree with those thoughts or statements. The real battle is lost if you begin to agree with the negative attitudes that have been caused by the abuse you have suffered. Naturally, at the start you have no one who will stand up and say, "Oh, that isn't right! You're not worthless, you are special!" You must therefore develop the skill of standing up and saying that for yourself and diligently seek God's help so that you will believe the truth.

Five Steps to Ridding Yourself of False Beliefs

Here are five important steps that can help sexual abuse victims in their recovery.

1. Identify the false beliefs that are blocking your path. The chart on page 69 is designed to assist you in this important first step. Each "false belief statement" in the lefthand column is contrasted with a scripturally based truth in the righthand column. All the statements in the first column are typical of those made by the many sexual abuse victims we have seen in therapy or read reports of in case histories. Search this list to see how many of these negative statements you may have said or thought about yourself.

2. Look for the roots of these false beliefs, the underlying factors that are causing you to maintain them. Which of these

---

*Minneapolis: Bethany House, 1980.

may have been introduced into your thinking by authority figures in your life (parents, teachers, other adults) or suggested by a perpetrator or co-perpetrator?

3. Recognize and accept these false beliefs as lies, and totally and finally relinquish them.

As you process the issues of having been a victim of sexual abuse, you may want to become part of a support group. Under the right circumstances, such groups (preferably Christian) can provide greatly needed encouragement, help you to achieve objectivity in examining your thinking, and challenge you to progress toward recovery. Because of the possibility of experiencing dangerously overwhelming flashbacks that group discussions may trigger, you are strongly urged to seek professional evaluation of your individual needs prior to and during participation.

Two further steps remain, and their importance to your total recovery can hardly be overemphasized:

4. Pray to God that he will wither away your false beliefs and reaffirm His truth about you.

5. Use God's Word, the Bible, to set you free from the deception of all the destructive falsehoods that have been holding you in their grip. Learn to take a stand, even argue against yourself, in order to develop a true belief system not rooted and grounded in sexual abuse. Learn not to be so harsh and critical of yourself, but rather to love yourself. We strongly recommend that, using 3x5 cards, you write out the affirming statements in the list of God's Truths on page 69. Keep them with you to use whenever they are needed. Remember, every statement in that list is based on scripture. Read them every day, and use them to reinforce your will to overcome all your false beliefs.

This part of your recovery is difficult, for you are possibly only now discovering the full extent of the devastation that sexual abuse has caused in your life. You are dealing with trauma that may seem more overwhelming than that which you experienced at the time of your actual abuse. Certainly that was true in my case—I believe I was even more afraid during my recovery than I remember being as a child in the darkness. Still, I knew that I was just then starting the process of becoming attached once again to those emotions and feelings I had had when my abuse was taking place in my childhood.

A Prayer for Perseverance

A prayer that I prayed for this part of my recovery may also help you:

> Dear Lord, Thank You for making me a prized treasure with a special plan for my life. Thank You that You have equipped me with everything that I need to achieve the goal that has been set before me. Thank You, Lord, that when I stumble, You lift me up; when I try to run away, You come after me; when I am defeated, You cause me to persevere to triumph. Thank You, Lord, for Your perfect love for me.

A Contrast in Beliefs

False Belief Statements	God's Truths
I am wasting my life.	God is able to provide direction in my life, and He is working in my life situation now and always.
I can't do it.	All things are possible with God.
I can't stand it any longer.	God is a source of love and patience to enable me to live a satisfactory and happy life.
I am dumb.	When I accept Christ, God equips me with the mind of Christ.
I am ugly.	I am beautiful and precious in the sight of the Lord.
People don't like me.	The Lord has given me attractiveness and love that I can demonstrate.
I am nervous.	Meditation on the Lord's unfailing love is a profound source of peace.
I'm plain and ordinary.	God has made me a very special person, someone exceedingly prized.
I'm just no good.	I am totally loved and accepted through Jesus Christ.
I am a failure.	Jesus helps me to overcome and triumph in all things.
I'm sick.	The Lord is the source of my health and healing.
I'm so tired and exhausted.	Confidence and joy in God bring me strength to persevere.
I am so lonely.	I am not alone, for the Lord will never leave nor forsake me.
I am so afraid.	The Lord's perfect love delivers me from any fear. The Lord has all power through which He delivers and protects me from the evils of this world.

False Belief Statements	God's Truths
I can't keep from thinking about food all the time.	The Lord invites me to present my body to Him as a temple for His Spirit and gives me the will to keep my body weight in correct proportion to my height and build.
My memory is so bad.	The Lord brings me insights for every situation through the memory of all He has done for me.
I never say the right thing.	The Lord will provide me with the gifts I need for carrying out His will.
I'm too timid and shy.	My trust in the Lord will bring me strength and confidence for whatever challenges I may face.
I hate myself.	God's unfailing love is sufficient to drive out hate.
I never can stick to anything.	God has promised to finish the good work that He has begun in me.

Statements like those in the first column of the preceding chart are things we say to express fallacious ideas of the sort itemized on the following page. As the counseling profession has been learning in dealing with victims of sexual abuse, when such ideas have once been introduced into a sensitized individual's mind, they are extremely difficult to blot out. Over and over, counselors have been sure they have totally convinced sexual-abuse counselees to give up the false belief(s) to which they have tenaciously been clinging, only to find upon their next session that they were wrong, and the whole process must be repeated.

False Beliefs Created by Sexual Abuse

1. The abuse was my fault.
2. I am hopeless.
3. I deserve to be punished.
4. I am helpless.
5. I am a failure.
6. I am not good enough.
7. I must please everyone.
8. Trusting people is dangerous.
9. I feel guilty.
10. Feelings are bad.
11. I am stupid.
12. People hurt you.
13. I must be perfect.
14. I am all alone.
15. I hate myself.
16. Everything wrong is their fault.
17. God abandoned me.
18. Sex is the way to get my needs met.
19. I can't say no.
20. My body is disgusting.
21. I can't be without him/her.
22. I must protect everyone.
23. Sex makes no sense; sex is violent.
24. I can't forgive.
25. If I am sexually unappealing, I won't be abused.
26. Parents/adults can do no wrong.

WORKBOOK

1. In Isaiah 24:11, the prophet describes the scene awaiting Israel: "There is a crying for wine in the streets; all joy is darkened, the mirth of the land is gone" (KJV). What special meaning does this verse have for you?

2. From the list of false beliefs on the preceding page, select the ones that seem to belong to you. Explain. You may have become aware of false beliefs other than those listed in this chapter. If so, state here, as clearly as you can, five of those beliefs (or fewer, if necessary).

3. Complete the word association quiz found on pp. 275–76, responding with the first thought that comes to mind, or moving on quickly to the next question without responding, if necessary. What insights did your responses give you; what surprises?

4. Select one false belief you have held that has noticeably affected your life and describe as fully as you are able the consequences of that belief in practical, spiritual, and emotional terms.

5. Explain how the following words of the Apostle Paul in his Second Letter to the Corinthians can apply in your life: "We demolish arguments and every pretension that sets itself up against the knowledge of God, and we take captive every thought to make it obedient to Christ" (2 Cor. 10:5, NIV).

6. Describe the roots that could have played a part in developing your false beliefs.

7. What false beliefs keep you from taking healthy risks in your life? Identify some of those risks and the positive consequences they could bring to you.

8. In Isaiah 40:24 (NIV), the prophet describes God's power over his creation:

> No sooner are they planted,
> no sooner are they sown,
> no sooner do they take root in the ground,
> than he blows on them and they wither,
> and a whirlwind sweeps them away like chaff.

How could that verse be applied in your life?

9. List what you see as the results you actually derive from the false beliefs you are maintaining in your life. How does it feel to maintain these beliefs, and what is it like to let them go? [More space for your answer at top of next page.]

10. Read the following passage from Colossians 2:6-8 (NKJV):

> As you therefore have received Christ Jesus the Lord, so walk in Him, rooted and built up in Him and established in the faith, as you have been taught, abounding in it with thanksgiving. Beware lest anyone cheat you through philosophy and empty deceit, according to the tradition of men, according to the basic principles of the world, and not according to Christ.

Compare being built in Christ with being built in the world. How does it feel to begin to rid yourself of false beliefs and build your life around God's truths?

6.

The Darkness and the Light—
Responsibility, Betrayal, and Denial

> "I will make darkness light before them,
> And crooked things straight.
> These things I will do for them,
> And not forsake them."
> —Isaiah 42:16b, NKJV

E very victim must deal with the issues of responsibility, betrayal, and denial. First and foremost, each victim must give total responsibility to the abuser. Unfortunately, from the moment of the first abuse incident, victims almost always become confused, losing their objectivity and normal reasoning abilities. Victims' descriptions of their first incident typically include such statements as "I was so confused"; "I don't know what I've done to deserve this"; or "if only I hadn't done this or that, it wouldn't have happened."

To Whom Does the Responsibility Belong?

Many of the rape victims with whom I have worked take the responsibility for the rape, at least in part. One fifteen-year-old victim said she had drunk too much. "It was a wild party. I knew when I went that there would be sex and alcohol. It is partly my fault. I just kept drinking and drinking. A couple of guys pushed me into this van. A couple more held me down—I'm not sure how many. Somebody told me it was eight.

"These were guys I went to school with. I couldn't go back to school for several days because I was so sore and bruised. And when I went back, everyone treated me differently. You know, if I hadn't gone to the party and drunk so much, all this wouldn't have happened to me. I knew those guys were partly to blame, too, but they had drunk a lot and they just wanted to have fun. Anyway, I didn't say no. In fact, I couldn't say no—I was too drunk." This young woman also received many comments from others confirming that if she just hadn't gone to the party, this would not have happened to her. The truth is that if she had not been the victim that night, someone else probably would have been.

Possibly if Jan, another rape victim, had not left fifteen minutes late from work and had to take the second bus, she might not have been a victim. But someone would have been. The four perpetrators who attacked her had raped before. In their own words, "We look for women that are alone." This particular rape took place in a populated area of a major city in New York State, and people passing by must have heard Jan's cries for help. It's too easy to shrug off such lack of response as being the norm for that area; the same thing has happened in Texas, California, and all across this nation.

What victims must begin to understand is that they were victims. *Webster's New Collegiate Dictionary* defines *victim* as "one who is injured, destroyed or sacrificed under any of various conditions," including rage, desire, ambition, etc. The fifteen-year-old described above was injured mentally as well as sacrificed for the pleasure of these eight young men. Responsibility for the abuse must be placed upon the abuser, not upon the victim.

When the Victim "Benefits"

Sherry tells me that her dad was really lonely. Her mom was mean and always griping to everyone. For as long as she could remember, she and her dad would escape together.

"He always said he was sorry for what happened, and I believed him," Sherry explains. "I really wanted to go with him every time he asked. We had so much fun—well, all except the sex. I hated it when he touched me, but I never hated him. I could've not gone, but I just learned to live with it. He gave me lots in return, money and special gifts. But most of all I felt sorry for him. It seemed to make him happy. Sometimes we'd have sex three times a day, but I just couldn't tell him no. So you see it was also my fault."

Sometimes victims received so-called "benefits" from the abuser, and Sherry's story certainly described some healthy ingredients for a relationship between a father and daughter. A father-daughter relationship should include good times, presents, and love. It should not include a role reversal between mother and daughter, and it should absolutely not include any sex. At some point, the victim must give the total responsibility to the perpetrator for the sexual offenses.

What about the Co-perpetrator?

The victim also must give responsibility to any co-perpetrator, that is, any individual who knowingly aids or allows the perpetrator to perform an abusive act. Certainly in a family setting with a mother present, her responsibility as a co-perpetrator must be recognized and dealt with. Victims sometimes express their greatest anger toward the mother in incestuous abuse. The child has learned at an early age that "mothers are to take care of their kids." Mother is usually the one who puts bandages on their scrapes and bruises. She usually dresses them, prepares their food, puts them to bed, and so on. So, why is she not doing something about what is happening? Often, the victim has to deal with the question of whether mother really knows or not.

Nevertheless, all victims must place upon the co-perpetrators their due share of the responsibility. Most co-perpetrators are not actively involved in the sexual abuse, but usually commit sins of *omission* rather than *commission*. Many times in family counseling sessions, mothers will weep over the fact that they noticed little things that weren't quite right, or just felt something was wrong but didn't know what it was. All seem to have come to the same decision to ignore or discount what they saw or felt was happening.

Other primary caretakers might have been too busy, too troubled, or victims themselves. The point is for the victim to acknowledge that others were responsible and to give that responsibility to all who should or could have been accountable; it is not for the victim to continue shouldering responsibility for the abuse.

Other Pieces to the Problem

Of course, there are many other pieces to the problem than dysfunctional or selfish caretakers who failed to protect their children, for example, our society's attitudes toward women, children, sex, and pornography. Sometimes such factors compel the victim to rationalize the responsibility of the perpetrator. Whatever may be involved, the perpetrator made the choice to abuse, and, in order for healing to take place, victims must show themselves to have relinquished responsibility to the perpetrator.

The Question of God's Responsibility

Victims must also deal with the issue of God's responsibility. Almost everyone who has been abused asks the question in one way or another. I cried out to Him again and again, "Where were You when this was happening to me?

You weren't there, and I don't feel You are there for me now." Ultimately God, of course, is responsible for everything since He is the creator of all.

Many victims describe a feeling of profound despair. "Why did He even let me be born? I would have been better off dead. Now to have this happen, why didn't He help me? Why didn't He kill my abuser? Where was He? I didn't do anything to deserve this." There are no easy answers to these questions, but there are answers.

Each victim must personally settle the issue with God. He is ready and willing to give you your individual answer. God states His position on sexual abuse in Leviticus 18. This chapter clearly sets forth the rules God intended for mankind's behavior. The penalty for sex with a child, or with a blood relative, and for rape all carried the death sentence. Psalm 115:16 (NASB) tells us that "the heavens are the heavens of the Lord; but the earth He has given to the sons of men." Now the question becomes, *Why did God give the earth to man, when He knew man was capable of great wickedness?* It seems that in God's master plan He wants a true love relationship with us, and this can only come about if we have free will to love Him or reject Him. If He forced us always to do right or be loving there would be no true love relationship—we would merely be robots and slaves who automatically act a certain way. Horrible suffering does occur on this planet because people use their free will to do terrible things to each other. God's unfailing promise in this setting, however, is to bring us through all abuses or problems triumphantly as we commit our lives to Him.

God Is Our Help

These questions can go on endlessly, but at some point, we must understand, as the psalmist says in verses 9–11 of the same psalm, "He is our help." Give mankind its responsibility and give God His. We live in a fallen world that will always have affliction, but God promises He will never forsake us or leave us. God will rescue our souls; He will keep our eyes from tears and our feet from stumbling.

Georgie, a beautiful woman in her forties, was ready to give up on God before she experienced the truth of God's promise. Now she is able to smile as she relays the anger she once felt toward God. "I would have choked Him if I could have. I felt totally betrayed. I would read all those passages and ask Him to help me. Nothing happened. I even prayed to die. Still, nothing happened. Finally I decided God was just a fantasy that weak people needed in order to get through life. Regardless of what God was called—Jesus, Allah, Buddha— no god anywhere heard anything. Then one day I really needed help and I prayed for His help. Something happened that day. Not much, but something. So I decided I would try to believe in God, as if He really worked. I began to pray for things in my life. Weeks, days, months, and yes, even years have passed and He does work. I also found a psalmist who agrees with me. Psalm 116:1–4, NASB, says,

> I love the Lord, because He hears
> My voice and my supplications.
> Because He has inclined His ear to me,
> Therefore I shall call upon Him as long as I live.
> The cords of death encompassed me,
> And the terrors of Sheol came upon me;
> I found distress and sorrow.
> Then I called upon the name of the Lord:
> "O Lord, I beseech Thee, save my life!"

Georgie ended her statement by saying, "And He did! He saved my life. He did not betray me; He saved me from the affliction of this world. I love the Lord because He rescued me from my past."

Victimized by Betrayal

God gave humankind a choice. All of us humans are accountable for the choices that we make on this earth. God gave us a manual, a rule book we call the Bible. Every victim's path has been crossed by an individual who chose the path opposite to God's direct command. You were betrayed, but you were not betrayed by God.

The word *betray*, in the Hebrew, occurs in a verb form that means "to *cause* to fall" or "to deceive, in order to betray." God does not deceive mankind, and there is not one word in the Bible that suggests a God who betrays mankind. His Word is given us to instruct us, to lead us and cause us to rise up and to be blessed. Abuse is not a blessing, nor is it a teaching. Rather, it is a betrayal by mankind. God redeems and restores.

According to Webster's Dictionary, *betray* means "to lead astray, to seduce by false promise, to desert in time of need." Truly a victim is often led astray by the effects of the abuse. Seduction is frequently a part of the victimization. Most important, a victim is deserted in time of need. A child in need of a healthy relationship with a parent is abandoned in the world of incest.

Many victims struggle with the issues of responsibility and betrayal. Others are engulfed in denial, refusing to recognize any of the effects that have been manifested in their lives. A young adult male told his counselor that he had been molested from the time he was six years old until he was fourteen. He didn't really like what had happened in the beginning, he said, but he stressed that he "was really bisexual." He didn't believe that this had any real effect on his life. He knew he was coming to see us for marriage counseling, but he assured us that being molested had nothing to do with his inability to be intimate. Besides, a long time ago he had worked through what had happened to him when he was a child. He knew what the Bible said about homosexuality, but of course that didn't really apply to him—he was bisexual. Anyway, it is a very difficult thing just to be heterosexual. Our society has a difficult time just abstaining from sex. Almost no one does.

The Trouble with Denial

The Hebrew word most often translated in the Bible as *deny* means, in its strictest sense, "to lie." If we apply that meaning, when we as victims of abuse deny our abuse, we are actually lying to ourselves. Often victims will tell me that they don't want to dig up the past, that they really are doing fine. Some will even quote Paul's statement in Philippians 3:13 to explain what they mean: "But one thing I do; forgetting what lies behind and reaching forward to what lies ahead. . . ." This is a great verse, but it does not mean that we should deny our problems. In fact, Paul spoke more about his past than any other person in the Bible. Moreover, in the earlier part of this same chapter of Philippians, Paul draws a most effective comparison between his past and what he later gained as a true servant of Christ.

In an individual counseling session, a woman was talking to me about her sexual relationship with her husband. "It can't be my sexual abuse. Before we married, I loved having sex. We had it all the time. It's that I don't love him anymore. I really hate sex with him. In fact, that's how I know I don't love him. . . . No, I haven't ever thought about sexual abuse. It doesn't affect me now. I got over it a long time ago."

The truth is that we can't put ourselves, God, or anyone in a box and close the lid on it. Perhaps there are some people whose earlier experiences of abuse have caused them few problems in their continuing life. This, however, is very rare. The cause for most people's denial is that they have detached themselves from their feelings. Victims of the violent crimes of rape and incest, regardless of their age, often shut down. This reaction is similar to that suffered after the shock of physical trauma, in which victims often recall that they felt no pain at first. Abuse victims understandably suffer an emotional shutdown as well as a shutting down of the physical pain. The body and the mind both have protective overload devices to be used in crisis. These are, however, intended for temporary use only; the longer they remain in place, the more damage they do.

A Case Study in Denial

During a session with her counselor, Gay, an eleven-year-old girl, described being forced to put her stepfather's penis in her mouth and having to suck it. She is quite detached from any feelings about what she is describing. She has a problem eating and seems sad in her appearance. She explains that she knows it's called a penis because that's what the child-protection lady told her.

She continues matter-of-factly, "At first I would spit out that stuff, but that made him mad. He told me, 'It tastes good,' but he lied. It tastes terrible. If there was a bowl, I would spit it in there, but he told me it was his juice. I had to do this four times each night. He lied, it didn't taste good, but he would hold his hand over my mouth and make me swallow it. He lied, it didn't taste good."

When Gay describes this absolutely terrible trauma which she suffered for a number of years in her young life, she displays almost no feeling but focuses only on the fact that her stepdaddy lied. Many questions such as "Did he hurt you?" "Did it smell bad?" "Are you angry?" "Are you sad?" and so on, receive inadequate responses. For Gay to survive when asked openly how she feels about her stepdad, herself, and her mother, there are almost no words. She wants to respond, but she appears lost and confused about expressing what she feels. Mostly, she looks perplexed.

If Gay grows to adulthood without any help, she will

continue to suppress her feelings. She was not allowed to object to what was happening to her. Her feelings of despair, horror, and betrayal were not validated by a significant adult. She was forced to evaluate her circumstance based on her perpetrator's lies, her emotional immaturity, and her dysfunctional surroundings.

Dissociation

A more complicated form of not remembering comes from dissociation. Persons in this condition have stored fragments of memories in bits and pieces in order to protect themselves from the overwhelming experience that would be produced by the complete recall of shattering events. A significant aspect of healing is gradually to recall the fragments and make appropriate connections. This frees them from being dominated by unwanted feelings and behaviors that are caused by dissociated memories. People cannot simply decide to remember, because the process is largely unconscious. However, in a safe environment, with an understanding counselor, they can gradually put the fragments of their memories together. Now they are no longer fighting nebulous forces and can work through the traumatic memories dealing directly with hurt, anger, grief, helplessness, or any other negative emotions.

As an adult, Gay will have a great deal of unresolved anger. She very well may display this anger in her relationships with others. She is likely to be overly critical toward others, and she may become an underachiever. Perhaps she will become an alcoholic or drug user. No one knows for sure what direction Gay's life will take. However, Gay is more fortunate than the many men and women who have suffered similar trauma but who will remain in denial and receive no help for their past sexual abuse. They will make such statements as "It doesn't matter," "It was a long time ago," and "I got over that."

A Time for Healing

The problem is that most victims don't just get over the effects of the abuse. It certainly doesn't just go away because it was a long time ago. The victims' denial of the effects of the abuse in their lives not only affects themselves but also their spouses, children, and larger family.

John 10:10 tells us that the devil comes to kill, steal, and destroy. One of the most effective ways evil can destroy an individual is through sexual abuse. If I take the responsibility that belongs to the perpetrator of the abuse, I will be consumed with shame, anger, and destruction that are not mine to suffer. If I truly believe God has betrayed me, I will not seek Him. If I stay in denial, the enemy will have stolen the deepest peace and blessings that God has for me. He will have stolen self-love and self-respect.

If you are the victim of sexual abuse, it is time in your life to give responsibility to the perpetrator, accept your betrayal, and come out of denial and thus begin the process of dealing with very painful memories. The process of healing has many ups and downs and proceeds at varying rates. If you were to remember all past events at once, you would likely be overwhelmed, but you must begin. If memories and feelings become too hurtful or tend to promote destructive behavior, then back off and rest. Once you are stabilized, you may safely resume the process.

A Final Caution

Before closing this chapter, a caution needs to be given: Be careful not to use denial as a way to avoid the truth. Yes, Christians are supposed to have forgiven their enemies and to be victorious. But until a victim of sexual abuse begins to deal with the principles of recovery, there is no hope for healing. Please, no longer deny the facts or hide in false responsibility. Allow God to take you beyond betrayal.

WORKBOOK

1. Can you think of any way you might have taken responsibility for your abuse? Describe the situation.

2. If you are the victim, who is the responsible party? How and why is (are) this person (these persons) responsible? Have you considered yourself a victim? How does it feel to think of yourself in that way?

3. Describe your feelings toward God regarding Psalm 27:10, "When my father and my mother forsake me, then the Lord will take me up" (KJV).

4. What part do you feel God played and will play in your abuse and recovery?

5. Read Psalm 115. Describe how this scripture applies or can apply in your life.

6. Describe what you have in common with the psalmist who wrote Psalm 116.

7. List the persons by whom you have felt betrayed as a result of your abuse. Describe your feelings toward your betrayers.

8. How do you feel you have protected yourself through the use of denial? Describe several ways.

9. Have you felt detached or dissociated from your emotions and your feelings? If so, describe any sensations brought about by that detachment. Describe how and when you shut down.

10. How would your life have been different if someone had validated your feelings concerning the perpetrator of your abuse and the abuse itself?

7.

Beyond the Darkness—
Principles of Restoration

He brought them out of darkness and
the shadow of death.
                        —Psalm 107:14a, NASB

Now that you have started your restoration from sexual abuse, it is important for you to understand the biblical principles of restoration. Knowing that one of the Hebrew words for *restoration* means "to live" provides a helpful image. For victims, restoration from abuse means "to live," perhaps for the first time in their lives. This same Hebrew word is also used with the meaning "to be restored to life."

From Death to Life

Victims have suffered a mental and emotional death from the experience of sexual abuse. They have been rendered incapable of living in the wholeness of body and soul that God created each individual to have. Now their first need is for their minds and emotions to be restored to life and health.

The specific word for *restoration* that is mentioned above can be found only in chapter 8 of 2 Kings, in a passage dealing with a woman who lives in Shunem. In 2 Kings 4, this Shunamite woman befriends the prophet Elijah, and she and her husband build a chamber for the prophet of God in their home. Elijah, wanting to do something for her, prays that she should conceive a son. The Shunamite woman gives birth to a son the next year. Later in chapter 4, the son, a grown man, has died, but God restores him to life. This story vividly demonstrates the principle of restoration: God gives life and even when circumstances cause death, God restores life.

God Will Restore

We must acknowledge that sexual abuse causes its own kind of death, but your next step is to begin to risk and believe that God will restore the life that has been stolen from you. The Shunamite woman appears again in chapter 8, where she has lost all her land holdings due to a famine. She appeals to the king, who has just learned from Gehazi, the servant of Elisha, that this is the woman whose son Elisha restored. The king then appoints an officer whom he commands, "Restore all that was hers and all the produce of the field from the day that she left the land even until now" (2 Kings 8:6b, NASB).

As all was restored to the Shunamite woman, begin now to believe that all can be restored to you. Begin your appeal to the King, Jesus Christ, and allow Him to restore you to life.

Help from Psalm 23

Another Hebrew word for *restore* is found in Psalm 23. This may be the most familiar passage in all of scripture to Christians and non-Christians alike. The Hebrew word for *restore* in verse 3 is used in a verb form that means "to cause [someone or something] to return and to restore [someone or something] to a former condition." This scripture can be a powerful part of your restoration.

In his book *God's Psychiatry,** Dr. Allen recommends reading Psalm 23 five times a day for one week to help with a distorted attitude about God, particularly that of viewing God as a remote, all-powerful judge. He explains the relationship between shepherd and sheep as the relationship between God and humankind.

---

* Charles Allen, *God's Psychiatry* (Old Tappan, NJ: Fleming H. Revell Co., 1953).

When Janice, an exceptionally thin blonde, first came into my office, she had very long, bouncy hair. She wore thick glasses and was always pushing them up, as they would frequently slip down on her nose. Once during that session, she acted as though she were going to spit. When I called God *Father*, she retorted very angrily, "This is what I think of my father." She stopped before actually spitting, but she had let me know in no uncertain terms that she couldn't stand thinking of God as "father." Every time she went to church as a child, she told me, she would think that God the Father was mean, just like her father. How she hated that word in any form!

I didn't see her for awhile, and one day she came to my office again. She had quite a different look about her. She had gained a little weight, and her glasses didn't seem to slip as much. She began to share a fascinating story.

"One day, I decided to give God one last chance," she said, laughing. "We are such egotists. I knelt down and cried out, 'God, I really need you; please help.' Something happened that was very special. I didn't know exactly what and certainly couldn't explain it. I still had a problem trusting this God—this father—so I didn't do anything like go to church or read the Bible. A few months later, I read a story in a magazine about a woman who had been in a car accident and who prayed Psalm 23 during her two years of recovery. This woman's story was so loving toward the Shepherd and so grateful for how he had helped her in all the physical and financial challenges brought on by the accident. She spoke of her victories with the Shepherd.

"Some time after this, I was asked to go to church with a friend. I went to her church three times, and all three times they taught on Psalm 23. My friend was completely embarrassed. But I knew in my heart it was just for me. Something happened to me that day when I knelt down and asked God to help me, but I couldn't do anything because even then the word *father* made me sick to my stomach. Now I see Him as

Shepherd, as Jesus. One day, perhaps soon, as my Shepherd continues to restore me, I will really see him as *Father*."

Psalm 23 is a powerful chapter for restoration from abuse. Verse 3 says, "He restores my soul." God does restore the soul, mind, feelings, and emotions. Often victims can't relate to God, and especially God the Father, during the early part of their recovery. Psalm 23 can help victims in starting a new relationship with God. The Shepherd will restore your heart, mind, and soul in spite of the scars that are left. Under Christ's Lordship, even the scars can help a person to become more compassionate, understanding, and resilient from having successfully survived such abuse.

More about Restoration

The Hebrew word for *restore* which is found in Joel 2:25 means literally "to make whole." That verse says God will restore to you the years that the locust has eaten, which can be interpreted to mean that God will make you whole by giving you back time. Most victims have had part or all of their childhood stolen. Often when victims survey the past, they are unable to see anything that is good.

No human could give back what was taken from your childhood. Only by God's touching your life can that really be done. If every perpetrator came and asked you for forgiveness, none could give you back the childhood he took. The fact that he has asked you for forgiveness may make you feel better, but only God can give you back the love that was stolen.

You can feel clean again. The shame, the filth, and the stain of abuse can be cleansed and replaced by the love and grace of God. Allow Him to touch all those areas where you need restoration.

I encourage you to follow your journey to complete restoration. Answer the questions at the end of the chapter and pray Psalm 23 every day. For the first week, pray Psalm 23 five times a day. Begin to believe in your restoration. Allow God to minister to you with this beautiful scripture (quoted here from the New King James Version). Read it as a prayer to Him:

> The Lord is my Shepherd;
> I shall not want.
> He makes me to lie down in green pastures;
> He leads me beside the still waters.
> He restores my soul;
> He leads me in the paths of righteousness
> For His name's sake.
> Yea, though I walk through the valley of the
>   shadow of death,
> I will fear no evil;
> For You are with me;
> Your rod and Your staff, they comfort me.
> You prepare a table before me in the presence
>   of my enemies;
> You anoint my head with oil;
> My cup runs over.
> Surely goodness and mercy shall follow me
> All the days of my life;
> And I will dwell in the house of the Lord
> Forever.
>   Amen.

God will not withhold his healing and help from anyone. He has restored me and many others who have taken the risk of recovery. He will bring you healing and restoration from the pain and hurt of loss and abuse.

Steps to Restoration

On pages 96 and 97 are twelve steps to restoration from sexual abuse. In my own recovery, the world had offered only the possibility of surviving. I did survive. I didn't commit suicide, but I ached inside every day. God offered restoration—new life. I didn't have these twelve steps written out, but these are the steps He took me through for my recovery. He taught me that there was much more than surviving, that there was also overcoming.

I hope that, from time to time, you will read these steps for direction and encouragement.

Twelve Steps to Restoration from Sexual Abuse

1. Acknowledge that you have been sexually abused and identify the effects that the abuse is having in your life.
2. Return the responsibility for your abuse to the perpetrator, co-perpetrator, family system, and/or any other contributing sources.
3. Acknowledge God as the source and power of restoration. Know that God is not the source of abuse but the solution to the trauma of that abuse.
4. Recount each experience of abuse by writing, talking, and sharing, again and again until the pain is gone.
5. Pray daily to identify and be restored from the sexual abuse, the passive abuse, the physical abuse, the emotional abuse, and the verbal abuse.
6. Work through denial, anger, guilt, shame, fear, betrayal, hurt, and loneliness, and learn to express your emotions and feelings.
7. Grieve over the suffering caused by all the things that were done to you and all the things you were forced to do. Grieve and release the pent-up rage at the lack of support and love that should have been there for you.
8. Place your worth, value, and esteem in the Word of God. Resist all guilt-producing, destructive self-hate messages from the world and from Satan. Find your significance in God.
9. Commit yourself to the biblical principle of forgiveness, and send away all hurts, despair, and agony of your abuse.
10. Allow God to cause your pain to be forgotten one day at a time, one memory at a time. Believe in Him and allow Him the time to restore your life.

11. With the support and guidance of a professional, decide whether or not to confront the perpetrator and other responsible persons. If direct confrontation is not advisable, express your feelings in a letter which may or may not be mailed after discussing it with your counselor.
12. Accept the fact that restoration will take time, but don't despair. Trust, peace, love, and wholeness will be yours. You have survived sexual abuse. Now overcome your trauma and go beyond the darkness.

WORKBOOK

1. Describe any feelings you have had that are similar to those of the Shunamite woman in 2 Kings 4:28 (NASB): "Then she said, 'Did I ask for a son from my lord? Did I not say, "Do not deceive me"?'"

2. List ten or more areas of your life which you want Jesus Christ to restore to you.

3. Do you think the Shunamite woman ever said, "Why me?" or, "If only things could have been different"? Have you ever thought those things? Describe any thoughts like these that you may have had, including the circumstances when they occurred.

4. After having read Psalm 23 five times a day for one week, describe how the Shepherd has personally ministered to you.

5. Read Joel 2:25–32; then explain what this scripture can mean to your life.

6. Read the Book of Ruth. What was restored to Naomi, the mother-in-law of Ruth?

7. Tell what Psalm 107:14 ("He brought them out of darkness and the shadow of death, and broke their bands apart" [NASB]) means to you.

8. Read the story of Joseph in the Book of Genesis (37:2–36; 39:1–50:26) and explain what it means to you.

9. Describe ways you may have been revictimized in your life. How has it felt to be a victim again?

10. Describe the hope that understanding God's process for restoration brings to your life.

8.

Sharing the Darkness—
Dealing with Shame and Guilt

For thou wilt save the afflicted people; but will bring down high looks. For thou wilt light my candle; the Lord my God will enlighten my darkness.

—Psalm18:27–28, KJV

Cathy describes in a counseling session how ashamed she feels about her body. "It feels dirty. It is dirty. As soon as my dad would get through with me, I would immediately take a shower, but I could still smell him, and I knew I had done something wrong. I felt bad. I felt guilty, as if someone was watching. I felt evil.

"Believe it or not, my pastor knew something wasn't right with me and my dad. He turned us in. I mean, turned him in. It stopped, but now it's ten years later and I still feel so much shame. I think I'll be okay and I'll get dressed up and ready to go out. Then suddenly a picture will flash in my mind of his sweaty body on top of mine, and I'll lose it. I'm totally devastated. I feel dirty and evil all over again. Sometimes I think that if I wouldn't have these flashbacks, I wouldn't feel so guilty. The truth is sometimes I feel ashamed for no reason. I just feel guilty for existing."

Every victim of sexual abuse is challenged by the need to recover from the shame and the guilt resulting from the experience. The shame is the feeling of humiliating disgrace at having been the victim of sexual abuse, while guilt is the terrible burden of "knowing" some great offense has been committed. In the process of recovery, victims must give back the shame to the perpetrator and wipe out the false sentence of guilt by overcoming their feelings of inadequacy at having failed to maintain acceptable behavior.

The Painful Emotion of Shame

First, let's look at shame as it is manifested in the lives of victims. This very painful emotion, which encompasses their minds and bodies, is planted in guilt, nourished by memories, and watered by secrecy.

"I know you tell me," Cathy continues, "that now that I no longer keep everything inside, I will get better. But it's been a secret so long I am afraid to tell! Listen to me! [She was starting to whisper.] I'll try to tell you everything I can remember. I promise, but not today."

Later, Cathy does go on to tell her story, again and then again. First she discloses it in individual sessions and then in a sexual abuse group. For Cathy, and for every victim of sexual abuse, telling the story is one of the most important and necessary events in achieving recovery.

Many victims, just like Cathy, begin to talk in a whisper as they speak about their experience of abuse. The initial disclosure is perhaps the most difficult challenge of the entire recovery process. Many victims have been threatened emotionally and physically that they are never to tell a word about what has happened. Many have been shamed into believing that if they were to tell, terrible things would happen to them or to someone close to them—perhaps their mother or sister. They have had to hear such things as "Everyone will know this is your fault," "Everyone will be mad at you," or "Mother will leave if she finds out." On and on go the menacing statements that victims are made to believe.

The Damage of Secrecy

Secrecy gives shame and guilt the power to torment victims. Secrecy isolates victims within their own minds and makes them believe that they are the only ones experiencing such devastating trauma. We spoke earlier of shame being like a plant whose existence depends on water. To use that metaphor in another way, not only plants but people must have water to survive. A human can live for many days without food, but only three days without water. To the victims of sexual abuse, secrecy is the water which the memories of the abuse depend on for their life.

Destroying the Strength of Harmful Memories

As victims are able to tell their stories, whether in a safe environment with pastor, counselor, or sexual abuse group, they can dilute and destroy the strength of the memories of the abuse. It is in disclosing the story that the ugly power of shame and guilt becomes apparent. In our analogy, the memories are the nourishment of the guilt.

The kind of toxic guilt and shame experienced in sexual abuse does not lead to godly conviction, repentance, and acceptance, but rather, to condemnation. Many Christians can quote Romans 8:1: "There is therefore now no condemnation to them which are in Christ Jesus." But reciting this scripture is not enough until we move its wisdom from our heads to our hearts. In my own life, every time a memory flashed across my mind, I would quote this scripture, then jot down a note to myself, and determine in my heart to tell this memory to someone. Eventually, the flashbacks became fewer and fewer; today I never have them. Occasionally I do newly recall some circumstance or incident from the innermost part of my being as God removes the obstacle blocking my consciousness. At these times, there is no condemnation, no shame, no feeling of inadequacy or of worthlessness. The memories are just that—memories, without guilt.

Dealing with Feelings of Inadequacy

Guilt is embedded in the feelings of inadequacy created by sexual abuse. Whether children of abuse or victims of rape, they received messages that say *You are not equal* or *You are not worth as much as I am,* and *My needs are more important than yours.* In other words, *You, the victim, are in fact helpless. You cannot really do anything to stop what is happening to you. And, even though you cannot stop the abuse, you are responsible, because it is happening to you and to no one else.* Feelings of inadequacy already fixed in the mind are further reinforced by these messages.

Gloria, a beautiful young woman of Hispanic origin, describes how she uses guilt to help her get things done with two small children and an ambitious husband. "I have a lot to do without much help at home. So whenever I get behind on things and feel depressed, I deliberately think about my abuse. I begin to feel sick about myself, and useless. Then, when I really need a boost of guilt, I begin to remember all the guys I slept with, and I start to cry and feel really bad. But it works, and I get everything done. It's like I punish myself and the penalty is to work real hard." Clearly the cost of this kind of motivation is destructively high.

Gloria continues, "I know, though, that the reason I am here and the reason I come to group is that I hope it will help my children. Also, my husband makes me feel guilty about everything. I know now that this is because I am so good at feeling guilty. In fact, I'm better than anybody at doing that. I realize that while using this guilt on myself makes me get things done, it also makes me feel really sad. The reason I beat myself over the head is because most of the time I just lie around and do nothing. I just don't have any energy. I guess I am depressed."

The Joy of Objectivity

Guilt often produces anger turned inward, which can lead to depression, as it did for Gloria. This is only one of guilt's many devastating effects on victims. To combat those effects, we urge that you begin by examining the areas of life where you feel guilty. It is often difficult to do this effectively, for sexual abuse robs us of our objectivity and leaves us feeling guilty about almost everything, even though there is no basis for doing so.

We did not commit a crime and we are not liable before the law; we were victims. Many adult victims and most child victims never make a sound while they are being subjected to abuse. They are frozen and unable emotionally to deal with the victimization. People are victims when they are unable to stop what is being done to them.

One victim is now able to laugh at herself as she describes her feelings of guilt. "First I feel that I am not doing enough for God; then I feel guilty about my husband. Next I overwhelm myself with guilt feelings about my children. Then come my parents. Finally I get to my dog and feel guilty because I don't spend enough time with her. After that I watch some talk shows and end up looking in the mirror and asking myself to forgive myself for not taking care of me."

As humorous as this story might seem to us, it illustrates an objectivity about our guilt feelings that is important to develop if progress is to be made. Examining our thoughts helps us to see if there are areas in our lives that God is convicting us to change. This kind of guilt, which is a grieving process leading to a change of heart, represents godly repentance. In Romans 2:4 Paul says that God leads us to repentance through His goodness. If we allow God to overcome our thoughts of guilt—deserved and undeserved—through His goodness, His path of freedom more than rewards us for the effort.

The Potter's Hand

Recovery may require relinquishing these areas of your life again and again to God. Most of us have read in the Bible that God is faithful and just; it is important to remember that we are dealing with a God who is also good. To repeat Romans 8:1, *there is therefore now no condemnation to those that are in Christ.* If you have never accepted Jesus Christ as your personal savior, take a moment to ask Him into your life. It will be the most important moment you have ever spent.

Romans 10:10 says, "All who call upon the name of the Lord will be saved." Salvation is ours for the asking. God will also save us from all our feelings of guilt and from the shame that controls us. He will set us free.

We receive further understanding from Jeremiah 18:4 (NKJV): "And the vessel that he made of clay was marred in the hand of the potter; so he made it again into another vessel, as it seemed good to the potter to make." A victim is marred by the abuser, and, as the potter did, the abuser makes a vessel that is full of shame, guilt, fear, and despair. But listen to Jeremiah 18:6: "'O house of Israel, can I not do with you as this potter?' says the Lord. 'Look, as the clay is in the potter's hand, so are you in My hand, O house of Israel.'"

Mankind mars the vessel of clay with the effects of sexual abuse, but God is the true Potter who takes the marred clay and makes it into a beautiful vase. He makes us into a vase full of life, full of value, full of worth. We begin to recover when we allow God to remake us.

A Further Look at Shame

Webster's Dictionary defines *shame* as "a painful emotion excited by a consciousness of guilt, shortcoming, or impropriety; disgrace, dishonor." The Hebrew concept of *disgrace* includes the idea of being physically uncovered, particularly the genital area; it can also refer to having one's plans and expectations frustrated or disappointed. Applied to the effects of sexual abuse, the description is amazing. Absolutely any form of sexual molestation, rape, or abuse carries the disgraces of the perpetrator. Often when victims tell the stories of their abuse, they are subjected to disgrace through looks and attitudes based on distorted concepts of abuse held by the listeners. "Why didn't you do something?" the victims are asked. Or they are told, "I knew someone had you before we got married!" "You coulda done something!" or, "It went on so long, you must have gotten something out of it."

Certainly the uncovering is a part of the abuse—the uncovering of the body as well as the uncovering of the mind. Innocence is destroyed and trust is lost. Memories of trying to cover one's body but not knowing how to settle one's mind come to the fore.

Just as certainly, victims of abuse are left with frustrated hopes and plans. Dreams for having a healthy relationship with a father, a mate, a mother, a brother, or a child have been demolished. A primary factor in shame is the belief of victims that they are insignificant, of no account, no good. As shame messages are exposed and overcome, victims will be less controlled, dominated, and poisoned by them.

The Perpetrator's Message

The shame message of sexual abuse springs from three major areas. The deliverer of the first of these messages is the perpetrator, who says, "What I want goes, and what is best for you is of no concern to me." These and all other messages that convey worthlessness are shame messages. Victims must begin the hard work of identifying the shame messages from the perpetrators and the co-perpetrators.

An adult female victim tells her story of abuse. "I was eight years old when it stopped. I'm not sure when it started. It stopped because my mom and step-dad got a divorce. I never fought, I never did anything when he would hold me close to him. I never did anything when he touched me except freeze and hope it would be over soon. I just felt bad. From the way people looked at me, I was sure everyone knew, and it made me feel guilty and useless. It happened again later with my stepmother, when I was a teenager. She said she was putting medicine on me. I would look away, down at the floor, sighing in hopes that she would stop touching me.

"I didn't know how to stop it. I couldn't tell anyone about my step-mom; it was just too bad. I told a pastor about my step-dad. What a joke that pastor was. He said, 'Don't you understand that your stepfather felt lonely and sad and all he wanted was some affection during the divorce?' 'Well, of course,' I agreed. But after that, I felt even more shame than before. I never told anyone else, that is, until now. But I am forty-eight now, and there are a lot of wasted years. I wish I would have known to tell and to keep telling until I found someone who would listen and believe me."

The shame imposed by the perpetrator's message is only alleviated by the wisdom of God. Paul wrote to the Corinthians in his first letter to them, "We do, however, speak a message of wisdom among the mature, but not the wisdom of this age or of the rulers of this age, who are coming to nothing. No, we speak of God's secret wisdom, a wisdom that has been hidden and that God destined for our glory before time began" (1 Cor. 2:6–7, NIV). Learn to speak God's word about yourself, not the perpetrator's damaging words about you. Learn to believe and give thanks to God. As the psalmist says, "I will give thanks to Thee, for I am fearfully and wonderfully made. Wonderful are Thy works, and my soul knows it very well" (Ps. 139:14, NASB).

Body Messages

A second area of shame has to do with feelings about one's body or body parts. Many victims see themselves as fat and ugly. Some purposely get fat or take little care of themselves in order to ward off further abuse. Some focus on a particular body part which they hate. Some are consumed with self-hate.

Twelve-year-old Kimberly tells her mother that she hates her body, all except her breasts. She likes starting to grow, but she feels bad about it for some reason. She thinks it's because when she was raped she didn't have any breasts and her abuser didn't touch that part of her. So it seems okay, but she feels confused. Sexual abuse develops in many victims a self-hate toward their body parts. Some victims hate stimulation of certain or all body parts by their mates.

This hate toward the body or toward the mind can be transformed by Jesus, as Paul points out in Romans 12:2 (NASB): "And do not be conformed to this world, but be transformed by the renewing of your mind [do not believe the message of shame, but rather God's wisdom], that you may prove what the will of God is, that which is good and acceptable and perfect." In other words, begin to understand that as Christ works healing, the abuse can no longer continue to haunt you.

Each memory, each thought, each negative message touched by God's restorative power overcomes the marring effects of sexual abuse. When you allow God to restore your soul from the effects of shame and guilt concerning your abuse, you can begin to embrace what God has already said: you are acceptable, good, and perfect.

Concealed and Unspoken Messages

A third area of shame can occur even without physical sexual abuse having taken place. Children—and adults, too—can be shamed by statements like "You can't do anything right" "You're stupid" or "You can't be my child." Being neglected also brings about shame. For example, if no one was ever home for you or cooked a meal for you, or acted as though they wanted you around, you probably felt insignificant and worthless.

Leave Your Burden with the Perpetrator

Shame and guilt are both great destroyers. If you feel a need to forgive yourself, please do it. Be cautious, however, to leave the shame and responsibility with the perpetrator. I felt the need to seek God's forgiveness from my abuse as well as from choices that I had made in my life based in faulty objectivity. Perhaps we just need to feel forgiven. "For you, O Lord, are good and ready to forgive [our trespasses—sending them away, letting them go completely and forever], and you are abundant in mercy and lovely riches to all those who call upon you" (Ps. 86:5, *Amplified*).

God says in Hosea 4:7, ". . . they sinned against me: therefore will I change their glory into shame." A perpetrator's sins are not only against the victim, but also the sin is against God. The shame belongs to the perpetrator.

In Isaiah 54:4 (NASB), God is speaking to the barren woman, Jerusalem, representing Israel in exile. What He says speaks to the victim of sexual abuse as well:

> "Fear not, for you will not be put to shame;
> Neither feel humiliated, for you will not be disgraced;
> But you will forget the shame of your youth,
> And the reproach of your widowhood you will
>   remember no more.
>
> "For your husband is your Maker,
> Whose name is the Lord of Hosts;
> And your Redeemer is the Holy One of Israel,
> Who is called the God of all the earth.
>
> "For the Lord has called you. . . ."

Give yourself and God the time to complete the good work He has started in you. This is a very difficult and painful part of your recovery that may take a long time. But please try to remember that even in the valley, God is with you. He will redeem the time.

WORKBOOK

1. List ten ways you have carried shame and write a paragraph about how it feels to do this.

2. List ten things you feel guilty about. Describe your feelings and your objectivity or lack of objectivity about them.

3. List five areas in which you feel inadequate and ten areas in which you feel adequate. How does it feel to make these lists?

4. Describe what Romans 10:10 (see p. 106) means to you as a victim.

5. Describe how memories of the past have added to or maintained your guilt and shame.

6. Describe your life of secrecy during the victimization and/or your life of secrecy after the victimization. How does it feel to have a secret life?

7. Describe your first experience of breaking the silence of your abuse.

8. Identify your feelings about the plans and expectations that were temporarily or permanently lost because of your experience of sexual abuse.

9. Contrast Jeremiah 18:4 (see p. 106) and Psalm 139:14 (see p. 108) by making two lists that compare what you felt you were with who you actually are.

10. Explain what Romans 12:2 (see p. 109) can and does mean in your life.

9.
Feeling the Darkness—
Anger and Hurt

And in that day they will roar against them
Like the roaring of the sea.
And if one looks unto the land,
Behold, darkness and sorrow;
And the light is darkened by the clouds.
—Isaiah 5:30, NKJV

Sara, a twenty-five-year-old black female, was expressing her feelings in a sexual abuse group. "I am angry at my brothers, I am angry at anyone who looks like my brothers. I am angry." For eight years Sara had been tormented by her brothers. She had been held down, tied up, and forced to imitate pornographic material. She described many humiliating and vicious acts perpetrated against her. She had made outcries, but no one understood. She is very angry about what happened to her as a child.

Almost everyone would acknowledge the right of the victim to be angry about being abused. Yet many of these same people would feel uncomfortable allowing victims the right to express their anger. Whether or not the perpetrator, co-perpetrator, the church, or the world offers the right to express anger, all victims have anger and need to learn to express their anger appropriately.

Expressing anger appropriately does not mean blowing up, throwing things, or using any form of violence. It does mean acknowledging, accepting, and expressing your anger in a mature and controlled manner.

A Preliminary Word of Caution

Before we proceed with the main focus of this chapter, a caution is imperative: If you are unable to use restraint in expressing your anger by harming others or yourself, immediately seek the help of a professional to explore all factors that may result in making it more difficult for you to deal with anger constructively. Lack of proper rest, physical problems, improper diet, depression, or being overwhelmed by memories of abuse can all impair the ability to cope with anger.

If you are prone to outbursts, you may find it helpful to meditate on Galatians 5 and the Book of Proverbs. Try to recognize any behavior patterns in yourself that have been learned from being around angry people. For example, if you had an explosive parent, you may well be imitating his or her uncontrollable temper. If you get "too angry," delay any response to the source of your anger and remove yourself from your circumstances until you have received professional counseling.

Giving Yourself Permission to Be Angry

Now, let's look at the need to give ourselves permission to be angry. Many victims might laugh at this idea because they consider themselves angry people, or are known as such. But the challenge lies in allowing oneself to give appropriate outward expression to the inner anger felt toward every perpetrator and co-perpetrator. This does not include taking it out on oneself or others who are not involved. The first question at the end of this chapter asks you to make a list of everyone with whom you are angry concerning your abuse. Yes, that list should include everyone from the actual perpetrator to all the co-perpetrators. Repeating our definition from an earlier chapter, a perpetrator is anyone who has sexually abused you in any way. A co-perpetrator is anyone who, by omission or commission, allowed the abuse to happen. Co-perpetrators can include parents, siblings, teachers, pastors, and protective services. It may also be important to consider the role of the legal system.

This last consideration is particularly important if you were molested as a child. For example, in many states children even as young as five years old are required to testify in front of their abusers. Victims who have gone through these types of circumstances have a great deal of anger over how the system revictimized them. A 36-year-old woman describes the experience of reporting her rape, the second by the same man. She had not reported the first assault because she thought it would be better if no one, including her husband and family, knew. Rather than being helped by the police on this occasion, she instead incurred accusations from them and eventually was encouraged by them to drop the charges.

It is most important, for these reasons, not to leave out one person, system, or organization when making your list of perpetrators and co-perpetrators. And don't be afraid to include God. Virtually every victim I have ever worked with has been angry with God. (I was so angry with God that I left the church for a few years and made a decision to be an atheist.) Last, but certainly not least, make sure you include yourself. You have probably been beating yourself over the head for years anyway, so put yourself on the list. Really take some time and allow God to reveal everyone toward whom you feel anger. Don't misdirect that anger toward those not involved or toward yourself alone.

Unproductive Forms of Anger

Anger is a part of God's nature, and the New Testament records that Jesus implied or expressed anger on several occasions. We can conclude that anger in itself is not bad, yet it is not appropriate to have a cruel and lasting anger like that expressed by King Ahasuerus toward Queen Vashti in Esther 1:12. This sort of unresolved anger inevitably causes us inner turmoil. The Bible admonishes us in Ephesians 4:26, "Be angry and yet do . . . not sin" (NASB). Most of us know how to be angry, but what we need to learn is how to be angry without sinning.

Anger, then, is a signal that God has given us, just as pain is a signal. Anger gives us a message that we are being hurt; that something is wrong, that someone is demanding too much. When we understand the simple dynamics of anger, it is obvious to us that victims of abuse have anger. They have been deeply hurt, and to remove that hurt, they become angry. They may express their anger in sudden outbursts, or it may be revealed in passive ways such as isolation or depression. The point is that these victims have displayed their anger in unproductive forms and will probably retain that anger until they can learn how to release it positively, and use it to find out more about themselves instead of lashing out against themselves and others.

The Hurt of Humiliation

We can become angry when we have been rejected, humiliated, or used, or when we have been hurt mentally, physically, or emotionally. All these hurts and more are included in the experience of a young woman who had been a child victim of sexual abuse. She described to me how rejected and humiliated she had felt as a young girl when the police came to her house. She had been walking home from school and had been approached by a man who "said he would give me candy. I never got candy, even though I went to the woods with him. He raped me. I was so sore, and blood was all over me. He tore my dress. A lady had seen me go with him, but it was over so quick. My mother got real mad at me and kept saying how could I be so stupid as to go anywhere with a stranger. She gave me a good weapon to punish myself. I was so confused. I didn't think anything could feel worse than when he did it, but this was worse. She's right, my mom's right. Why did I go into the woods? I *was* stupid. I hate myself and I am very angry with myself."

The Danger in Denial

Some victims disclaim any emotion of anger. "No, I'm not angry at my mom; she just didn't know it was going on, that's all!" Others say, "Well, it was so long ago, it doesn't matter any more," while still others claim, "I forgave the person and just put it in the past." Certainly God is full of miracles, but most people need to process the trauma of this childhood experience and not push it under the rug—not even a spiritual rug. Anger that is not dealt with will come out through inappropriate depression, psychosomatic ailments, relentless shame, and guilt.

Anger Turned Inward

It is tempting to allow anger to become bitterness. Genesis 4:5–6 relates that "Cain became very angry and his countenance fell. Then the Lord said to Cain, 'Why are you angry? And why has your countenance fallen?'" (NASB). This kind of anger turned inward becomes depression. We can make one of three choices with anger: (1) we can turn it to the outside where we blame everyone for all the bad things that have happened to us; (2) we can turn it inside and blame ourselves for these things (either of these two choices will eventually lead to emotional destruction); or (3) we can learn to express our anger with God-given biblical principles. Clearly the third choice is best for our emotional and spiritual health.

This time in your life—the time of recovery—is one in which you can express your anger. You no longer need to hold it inside you in order to survive. I once asked a young man, "How can you keep the schedule you do?" His reply was that he had so much hate and anger inside from having been abused as a child that it gave him the energy to get up every day at 5 a.m. and go until midnight. He did, however, complain about headaches, stomach problems, and an occasional rash; but he insisted that he needed his anger, that it was a friendly companion. The young man was partly correct. Anger is an ally, but not a helpful one when characterized as a silent rage inside.

As this story suggests, it is a fact that the effects of child sexual abuse can lead to chronic anxiety, eating disorder, multiple personality disorder, depression, promiscuity, alcoholism, and a host of other problems. It is a fact that if you had not been abused, your life would have been different. You could have been more confident, less angry, and more stable in your personal behavior.

But the reality with which you must deal is that you were deeply hurt by your abuse, and you do have a great deal of anger. You may need to appropriately express your anger again and again and again until you have been released from the rage within.

Group Support for Survivors

Anger may at first have seemed to help many of us survive our abuse and to keep us going, but now it is time to grieve over the hurt and direct the anger appropriately. I strongly urge you to find a support group for sexual abuse survivors under individual therapy. If this is impossible, please find someone who can help you process the pain of your trauma, and who understands the issues of sexual abuse. When I was beginning my recovery, I told many professionals about my experience, but at the time none really knew how to help me. So, if there is absolutely no one, remember, there is God. Even though it appears to you that He was not there at the time of your abuse, He was. He was sad and angry over your abuse. Nobody wants justice more than God. Please reach out to Him and allow Him to touch you and to help you. Remember, He died for justice.

Dealing with Hurt

As we have noted just above, a primary cause of anger is hurt. In order for us to deal with anger, we must also deal with the hurt that is at its root. According to Webster's Dictionary, *hurt*, as a verb, means "to cause harm, physical injury, or damage; to impair the value, usefulness, beauty, or pleasure of something; to wound the feelings of someone or to distress." In sexual abuse, the hurt—the wound or injury—takes the form of mental, physical, and emotional pain. The hurt you experienced was the harm, the evil, and the damage done to you as well as the betrayal and loss of innocence you suffered.

We must acknowledge *all* the hurts, no longer denying, discounting, or minimizing the effects our abuse has had upon us, but learning instead to make anger a valuable ally. As we find the roots of our anger and hurt and are helped by God's Word, wise counseling, and the support of other abuse victims who have preceded us in our journey out of the darkness, we will find more appropriate and constructive ways to express it and grow in our relationship with others and with God. Even though we may become very discouraged and not want to go on, we can push on with Christ. We can survive one more day and one more day until we overcome.

Passive Abuse

Another very real form of abuse that victims may have suffered is passive abuse—neglect. That kind of abuse occurred in all the times when no one was there to put them to bed, to say "I love you," or to hold them when they fell down. It was there in all the times the wrong words were said and in all the times of silence when no words were spoken.

As Ezekiel 16:5 laments, "No eye looked with pity on you

to do any of these things for you, to have compassion on you. Rather you were thrown out into the open field, for you were abhorred on the day you were born" (NASB). Acknowledge the evil, the loss, the damage that was done to you, not in self-pity, but in God's pity. Understand that you must risk remembering the pain so that you will no longer need anger as your protector. God says in Ezekiel 36 that He will sprinkle clean water on you and you will be clean. God says He will remove the heart of stone from your flesh and give you a new heart. He will put His spirit in you and you will be His child and He will be your God.

Where Is God?

Many victims wonder where God was in the midst of their abuse. As I've said before, there is no easy answer. But I believe God asks us to seek His wisdom on all questions. Many victims have held onto a belief of something good even in the midst of the abuse. Some struggle with the question "Why does evil exist?" Others have cried out to God from the time of the abuse to the present. Some speak of seeing Jesus or of some miracle that seemed to have taken place right in the middle of their abuse, while others have simply had a hope of something good about life. It seems that many were unable to let go of this hope, no matter what was done to them or what they did themselves. They never stopped hoping in good.

I am convinced that this belief, hope, and desire was God. Even though we may not have been aware of it, God was there, there in the belief deep in our souls of something good. He was there when we were being abused. He was there in our loneliness. He was there in our pain. He was the one who taught us to hope.

Isaiah 53 describes Jesus as a man who was despised and forsaken by men. The New Testament tells of Jesus being spat upon, beaten, and mocked. As we know, all sin came upon

Him when He was on the cross. He has borne all pain for us, even the pain of sexual abuse.

Give Jesus your heart one memory at a time, one hurt at a time. Allow Him to set you free from all the effects of your abuse. Allow Him to hold you as a baby. Allow Him to hold your hand. Remember that He prepares a banquet for us in the presence of our enemies. Wherever you hurt, allow Jesus, our God, Jehovah Rapha, to heal you. He is the God who heals us. He is the God who paid the price and walked the walk we walked. No one hurts for your loss more than Jesus does.

The Therapy of Writing Letters

After you acknowledge your hurt, take the list of perpetrators and co-perpetrators you have made and write each of those persons, organizations, or systems a letter that you do *not* mail. Take these letters and read them to a group, a trusted individual, or an empty chair. Then, write God a letter expressing your anger. In the past I thought, *I can't express anger toward God*, even though I would whisper thoughts in my mind. He, of course, knows exactly what we are thinking and feeling, whether those thoughts are angry or happy.

Some of my letters had to be written two or three times. You will probably find, as I did, that as you process anger in one area, God may bring additional issues to mind. Remember, recovery takes place one day at a time, and if need be, one letter at a time.

Sometimes it may be necessary to write a person who is already dead. This is quite appropriate since none of these letters is to be sent. They are simply tools to put you in touch with your anger and hurt. I often recommend that these letters to the deceased be written as good-by letters. If you feel you can't handle writing a letter to a deceased person, write to Jesus and ask Him to deliver the message.

Since these letters will never be sent, and because writing

them is a major step in recovery from anger, it is extremely important that you be absolutely honest about what you say. You may have been carrying some of these feelings since you were three or four years old. Don't leave out anything, and don't express your anger about just the sexual abuse, but also about the passive abuse.

Accept the challenge. Express yourself honestly and allow your anger to be a healthy part of your life. Reading the Psalms helped me to accomplish this important step in my recovery. I picked out the ones that cry out, "Come quickly," "How long, O God, will you turn from me?" and so on. Finally, I just lay flat on my face and vented my pent-up feelings. "Oh, God, where were you? Why didn't you help me? You were all I had to believe in. You failed me. You betrayed me. Surely you could have done something. Why didn't you?"

I wept for a long time. Nothing seemed to happen. I didn't hear angels singing or trumpets blowing. I just felt better. I got up, and after a time, I realized I *was* better. And I wasn't so angry. [For a similar experience read Lamentations 3.]

Finally, I wrote a letter to myself containing all the false and real accusations against me. I wrote about all the times I should have known better than to act as I did and the times I believed that what had happened was ultimately my fault. I recounted all the mistakes I had made as an adult, whether or not they were a result of the abuse. Over and over, I expressed my anger toward myself until I finally began really to believe in Romans 8:1: "Therefore, there is now no condemnation to those in Christ Jesus." I accepted myself.

The Message of a Nail Print

Rosaline, a bright 35-year-old nurse, full of intellectual humor, described her anguish about her hurt. "If Jesus had really felt my hurt, surely He would have helped me. The pain of the abuse was overwhelming. The complications of my life were overwhelming. I was full of anger and frustration. I couldn't sleep.

"This is how I have felt most of my life. One night I woke up at about 3 a.m., troubled, knotted, and worried. I went for a walk and just started crying. I said, 'God, I am trying to believe you love me . . . I want to believe . . . help me to believe in You.' Then the thought entered my mind that Jesus was holding my hand, and I could feel the nail print in His hand. In one moment, I *knew* He felt my hurt. In fact, He felt my pain so deeply that He took the pain upon Himself.

"I looked at my hand and clasped His in mine. I knew He loved me—the nail print said just how greatly He loved me. I began crying at the joy of knowing and feeling His love. I felt God was saying to me, 'Yes, see how I love you.' I felt so loved and so encouraged that I knew everything would be okay."

WORKBOOK

1. Make a list of every perpetrator, co-perpetrator, organization or system that you feel has hurt you, let you down, and/or toward which you feel anger.

2. Isaiah 5:30 appears just below the title on the first page of this chapter. It is reprinted here for your convenience.

    > "And in that day they will roar against them
    > Like the roaring of the sea.
    > And if one looks unto the land,
    > Behold, darkness and sorrow;
    > And the light is darkened by the clouds."

    Explain what this verse means to you and describe your feelings in reading it. Why is it appropriate as an introduction to this chapter?

3. Write out three incidents from your past that you feel most angry about.

4. Explain how you believe you have been expressing your anger. Do you suppress it? Does it show itself in sudden outbursts? Depression? Self-hate? Passive-aggressive or self-destructive behavior? In what other ways?

5. Describe how you react to anger that is directed toward you.

6. Describe any problems you have in expressing your anger.

7. Look up the word *anger* in your dictionary, and list the definitions that match your feelings.

8. Describe the passive abuse you have experienced in your life. What successful strategies have you used to deal with both active and passive abuse?

9. On separate sheets of paper, write letters to your perpetrator, co-perpetrator, yourself, and God, expressing all the anger you feel.

10. Write a letter to Jesus, giving Him all the hurt and pain of both overt and passive abuse.

10.
Living in the Darkness—
Healing Loneliness and Fear

For God did not give us a spirit of timidity,
but a spirit of power, of love and of self-disci-
pline.

—2 Timothy 1:7, NIV

How can I or anyone describe the loneliness of abuse?
How can I describe the terror, the despair, the deso-
lation of the nights and the days? How can anyone touch
the forsakenness of a victim? Can anyone really describe the
horror of dwelling in darkness?

I listened to a child say to herself, "There is no one to turn
to. No, there is no one. You must obey your father. He says
you must be a good little girl. What is wrong with you? Your
daddy comes just to see you. You be nice to him. You take care
of Daddy."

What is it like to be this child? Fear and loneliness surround
her waking thoughts. She despairingly asks, "How can he
have sex with me at night and act normal the next morning?
How is it he can do that? I keep looking at him just to see if in
some way he will give me some sign. No, he just acts normal.
Just like nothing happened last night. This scares me. I must
be crazy, because I don't feel normal. Normal—how can he
act normal? Why doesn't he even ask how I am? I told him it
hurt. He told me to shut up. Maybe he will ask me in a minute
how I am.

"I know what he said to me is true—that anyone I told about it would say it's my fault. Just the same, I think I'm going to tell my teacher today. She likes me. I think my grandmother knows. Why does she think he is so great? Oh, I guess I won't tell my teacher today after all. Daddy said I would be in bad trouble, real bad, if I tell anyone anything. He slapped me across the face and it left a mark. No one even noticed. I guess I won't tell today, but maybe tomorrow. I feel so scared!"

Fear and Abandonment

One story, one life, but thousands of lonely and desperate days. In my counseling, I hear many stories from many more lives, with different details, but all repeating the same theme of fear and abandonment.

A teenager struggles to get out her words: "I can't go to school. I don't know why; I'm just afraid. Sometimes when I turn the corner at school, I think I see my rapist's face. Then I look again and it's someone else's. He doesn't even go to my school.

"It only happened once, two years ago. Why can't I just forget it? It was in the summer—my brother's friend. He raped me in my butt. I just can't stand the thought. When I even think of it, I want to run, to just get out of here. I can't even breathe. I'm not going to school. I'll tell my mother I'm sick. I can't spend the night with anyone any more. I just want to be at home. I just want to stay in my room.

"I have an emptiness all inside me. It's like a big hole, as if you'd look at me and you couldn't see my middle. He took my middle that night. I didn't say a word. I just let him. It's like I was motionless. I think I was in shock. Maybe that's why I didn't move. I pretended I was asleep.

"I sure can't tell anyone now. It's been too long. When I see him anywhere, he just smiles this sickening smile. My brother isn't his friend any more, but it's like this creep knows how afraid I am. He smiles like, *Don't look at me; you liked it! You just took it and never said a word.* I can't go to school. I can't go anywhere!"

One male victim told of being left with foster parents when he was in the sixth grade. At the time, he hated them, but later, in recovery, he realized they were just simple, nice people. During his stay with this family his sixth-grade teacher molested him. He told me that no one seemed to notice or to care much when the teacher would take him places. "It felt good, but I felt dirty," he said. "I hated kissing him. All I thought about was sex. I started masturbating several times a day, and I would try to touch every girl I got around.

"I finally left the foster home and went to live with my dad. I graduated from high school and a couple years later, I got married. It was easy to get sex in high school and college. There was always plenty of sex. Even after I married, I slept with everyone I could. I felt driven to prove my masculinity, I guess. I needed to be known as a man who got the women.

"But then I got saved, and something inside me was different. I actually began to love my wife. I began to see the tragedy of my life. I saw the fears—fear of being alone, fear of homosexuality, fear of life. It took a long time for God to work with me, but finally I was able to receive His help. I don't have perverted thoughts or do unspeakable things any more. Now, I'm not afraid to face life. I don't have to be macho or even prove I'm okay."

The Urgency of Protection

Many victims have a great deal of fear of their perpetrators. Often, they refuse to be around the abuser. This is the best approach even when the perpetrator is a family member. Every effort needs to be taken to protect victims. The next story is a case in point.

A 25-year-old woman with a sweet southern accent tells of being attacked by an older family member: "He had already tried six times, but he'd never really touched me. I fought so hard, I always got away. But then one night he came in my bedroom and grabbed me and put a washrag over my mouth. It had a terrible smell. I began to feel sick at my stomach, and my head was spinning. I'm not really sure what happened, but when I woke up later, I could still smell my vomit even though it had all been cleaned up.

"It never happened again, but almost every night for a long time afterward I would wake up terrified. I would think that someone was holding me down and putting chloroform over my nose. I would feel so helpless, so alone and afraid. I'd lie there silently, hoping my breathing wasn't making a noise, and I wouldn't move because I knew if I did, even the tiniest bit, something bad would happen."

Losing one's fear of perpetrators may require a long recovery process, depending on the victim, the abuse, and the perpetrator. For Belinda, an eleven-year-old girl abused by three male perpetrators, it has taken more than three years just to overcome her fear of men. Two of the perpetrators had anally, orally, and vaginally raped her. Both at some time during the abuse had tied her up, threatened her with violence, and taunted her about getting her pregnant. When asked to draw pictures of her perpetrators, she showed them as black figures with mean faces. She drew all men in this same fashion, whether or not they were perpetrators.

After long-term counseling and a change in family structure (new stepfather and baby brother), her drawing of the family portrait changed slightly. The non-perpetrator stepfather and the baby brother were still shown as black figures, but in the midst of the picture, the infant was wearing bright green clothes. The difference in the drawing was slight, but it signified a major step in the recovery. At the writing of this book, Belinda has asked to go with this loving stepfather on a couple of short errands.

Another reaction caused by her abuse was that, during her mother's pregnancy, Belinda became quite concerned that she too might be pregnant. Even though at least three years had gone by since her abuse, this deeply embedded fear had been triggered by her mother's pregnancy.

Every victim's story contains the issue of fear. Some of these fears are very rational; others are not. Obviously, God wants us to have wisdom and general respect for the reality of life's circumstances. For example, if I am wary of jogging alone at 10 o'clock at night in a major U.S. city, that could hardly be considered an irrational fear. But, if I am afraid to take a desirable job in a reputable area across town, I need to discover whether it is simply because the job is inconveniently far from home, or whether there are deeper fears that I need to overcome. I can accomplish this through telling my story and sharing my feelings with a counselor, a recovery group, or a meaningful friend, and by all means, claiming God's redeeming, healing promises.

Compensating for Fears and Loneliness

There are many ways of trying to compensate for our fears and loneliness. We may minimize the problem or even deny we have one. We may try to do everything for everyone and have our needs met through the approval we receive. We could attempt to be perfect, to have a perfect home, perfect children, and a perfect spouse. We could choose anger as a shield to protect ourselves from experiencing the reality of our fears. Some of us may attempt to be in total control of our circumstances or even become daredevils, taking up skydiving, motorcycling, and other risky activities. Other ways to compensate include eating or drinking everything in sight or endlessly shopping for bargains; withdrawing and isolating ourselves; or by contrast, giving total devotion to church or volunteer work, serving day and night in every conceivable role.

But no matter how many of a million and one things we try, we are destined to discover that only God's plan will work.

He is the deliverer. He is the restorer. We must face our fears and loneliness by telling our story to appropriate others and releasing those burdens to God.

Restoration from Loneliness and Fear

Let's deal first with loneliness. For God to rid us of the problem, we must acknowledge each lonely feeling, one by one, and hand it to God. We must do the same with all the ways we've compensated for those lonely feelings and the ways we've survived one more day. And we can pray again Psalm 51:6, asking God to leave no stone unturned in revealing the truth of our loneliness.

This process will probably be painful. In my own life, I remember never having hurt so much as I did during the recovery process. In typical fashion, to survive the terror of the moment, at first I shut down. But I knew no matter how much it hurt to remember, I would have to try. It did hurt very much and for a long time. But one day I woke up and realized that the pain wasn't quite as intense. Then the next week, it was even less. The next month, other memories no longer hurt, and so on until one day I felt whole.

The psalmist assures us, "For thou wilt not leave my soul in hell; neither wilt thou suffer thine Holy One to see corruption. Thou wilt show me the path of life: in thy presence in fulness of joy; at thy right hand there are pleasures for evermore" (Ps. 16:10–11, KJV). Loneliness and abandonment are the condition of a soul in hell, but God is willing to show us the true and joyous path of life. As you begin to pray specifically for your restoration from loneliness, allow God to touch that emptiness and fill your soul with His love. You may want to pray Psalm 23:3, asking Him to restore your soul.

The next important step is to overcome the invasion of fear in your life. For this you will need to receive God's help in alerting your mind to the reality of the present. You can deal with irrational fears by submitting them to God, one at a time, and receiving His restoration from abusive situations. This process takes time, of course. And it also takes seeking and accepting accurate information. For example, Belinda, the young teenager we described earlier, was eventually able to recognize intellectually that someone cannot be pregnant for three years.

Another realm of fear with which the victim must deal is the spiritual. We are told in 2 Timothy 1:7 (KJV), "For God hath not given us a spirit of fear; but of power and of love and of a sound mind." There are very few places in the Bible that actually say "spirit of" something. Among them, in addition to "spirit of fear" in the scripture just above, are "spirit of jealousy" and "spirit of heaviness." Since this kind of phrase occurs so rarely, we would probably be wise to recognize its importance. Many abuse victims describe a strong feeling of a presence of evil. Some tell of experiencing a fear so great that even outsiders looking in those persons' eyes could see this terrifying stare. We are in great need of the "spirit of power and love and a sound mind" referred to in 2 Timothy 1:7.

Wherever you are theologically, please consider and use the many scriptures God has provided for our deliverance. Remember Romans 8:15, "For the spirit which you have received (is) not a spirit of slavery, to put you once more in bondage to fear, but you have received the spirit of adoption—the Spirit producing sonship in (the bliss of) which we cry Abba (that is) Father" (*Amplified*).

The Fear of Abandonment

One root fear that most victims must process is the fear of abandonment. Once when I was doing self-esteem group therapy for teenagers in crisis, a beautiful sixteen-year-old female of Indian heritage entered the circle. I saw how tense she was, and I was stunned by the relentless, distant stare of longing in her eyes. She soon related that she was pregnant with her father's child. She had run away from home to keep the baby, but she said she hated this yet-to-be-born life. She moved and talked like the rest of us, but never before had I seen such hopelessness in a person's eyes. How could anyone help her make sense out of her life? At this time, all we could do was help get her through the pregnancy and delivery. In her view, there was no mother, father, husband, or God. She couldn't kill a life, but she really didn't know why because life, to her, wasn't worth living. In her opinion, if there really was a God, He had very little worth. She felt abandoned, and she was abandoned, by the world.

The sexual abuse victim's fear of abandonment is like that of someone left in a forest alone, confused, and in pain. It is dark and there are many dangers in the forest. Fear grips you and there is no one to whom you can turn for help. If you walk straight ahead, you're afraid of the danger that faces you, yet turning back may be just as risky. You know you must go on, but a part of you, or maybe even all of you, is overwhelmed with fear and just wants to sit there and die. But even that thought frightens you.

In recovery, although it may seem that you are still in the forest, you have found the way. Identifying your fear of abandonment and feelings of loneliness, then facing these realities, is the path out of the forest, even though it may be a long one.

The Fear of Harm

Other victims speak of fears for their safety: A young child tells me she knows that Daddy can't see her for one year because the law said so. But she explains that when she goes to bed at night, she's afraid just the same. She thinks that Daddy will come across town, climb over the fence, crawl across the backyard, and then come in her window and get her.

Another child, six years old, forced to testify against her abuser, explains to me that she knows the judge will be there and the jury will be there. One, two, three . . . twelve of them.

The police will be there, but her abuser will be there too, and when no one else is looking, he will fall down on the floor and crawl past the jurors and the judge and come behind the witness stand and get her.

Such fears are very real to these children, although they may seem groundless to an adult. Adult victims at times do not remember or recognize the fears related to their sexual abuse. Instead, adult victims often experience their fear indirectly, unspecifically, and unexpectedly. In these cases, their feelings have become separated from their cause; in technical terms, they are suffering from dissociation.

Fear of the Unknown

Adults may have tension or anxiety of unknown origin. They may feel uneasiness or be afraid to do things. One adult victim describes walking into an airport and becoming so anxious that she found herself running to the seating area and collapsing into an empty place in the corner. She doesn't know why; she was just so afraid. Others speak of being afraid of large crowds or of being alone; of being scared of spiders, snakes, people, authority figures, and a host of other things.

Many victims have problems sleeping, often because of terrible nightmares. One victim told me she frequently dreams of spiders and of dead people. She's not sure if she is dead in the dreams, but there is no one to help her. Another victim describes shadows as black spots. She tries to see into them, but there isn't anything there. At first she thinks she's seeing bugs, but when she looks again, she sees nothing.

Some people tell of waking up at night feeling terribly afraid. One victim says it's as if there are twenty Boston stranglers outside the door who are about to come in and get her. Another has a terrible fear of thunderstorms. "I know it doesn't make sense, but I can't stand it. I have tried to figure it out, but I am so afraid." Still another victim describes her fear of being closed in. She can't be on elevators. She will walk up ten flights of stairs if she has to, rather than get on an elevator, where she fears she can't breathe.

The Bondage of Fear

Truly, if we are in fear, we are in bondage. We are slaves to those thoughts and those actions which we think will gain us peace. It does no good to run away from fear or to ignore it or try to compensate for it. We must seek competent help and use the Word of God and the comfort of His people.

Perhaps right now you are in too much pain or fear to do anything about your situation. If so, I urge you to memorize one or more of the scriptures suggested here. They offer solid help in many situations, especially Jesus' loving words in Matthew 11:28 (NASB): "Come to Me, all who are weary and heavy-laden, and I will give you rest." When fear comes upon you, James 4:7 (*Amplified*) is of particular support: "So be subject to God—stand firm against the devil; resist him and he will flee from you." We are assured by 2 Samuel 22:2 (RSV) that "the Lord is [our] rock and [our] fortress and [our] deliverer." Pray the Lord's prayer every day. When you pray the words of Matthew 6:13, "but deliver us from evil," really apply this request to any fears you have.

At one point my own life was so full of fears that I isolated myself from practically everybody. In my freshman year at college, I would eat my lunch in the third-story bathroom of the library. Not many people ventured there, so I was alone and I felt safe. The truth is I was afraid of people.

It's been years since I had those fears, but I can sympathize with you. Wherever you are, you can begin the process of overcoming your fears.

The Comfort of God's Restoration

As you allow God to know your fears, His love can restore to you all the days of anxiety you have endured. If you have a heart full of holes and marked with bruises, He can take that heart and make it whole.

One victim who couldn't see anything good about her childhood marveled after recovery at how God could draw forth memories of good things—memories so buried in sorrow she had lost them. Another victim in my sexual abuse group laughed one day, "I must be getting better—I am remembering funny things about my childhood."

No one loses the reality of past loneliness and abandonment, but in the recovery process God redeems the time spent in that condition. He causes the present to be full of His love, His joy, and His peace. Just below is 1 Corinthians 13:4–8a (NASB), a most beautiful and comforting scripture. First read it as is. Now go back and read it a second time, replacing the word *love* with the word *God*. After that, read it a third time with the word *I* instead of the word *love*. Please remember in your recovery process that God *is* love. God never fails. Love never fails. He will never abandon you.

> Love is patient, love is kind, and is not jealous; love does not brag and is not arrogant, does not act unbecomingly; it does not seek its own, is not provoked, does not take into account a wrong suffered, does not rejoice in unrighteousness, but rejoices with the truth; bears all things, believes all things, hopes all things, endures all things. Love never fails. . . .

WORKBOOK

1. Read all of Psalm 143 from your favorite version of the Bible. Describe what this psalm can and/or does mean in your life, particularly verse 3.

2. Describe what you have said or now say to yourself, aloud or silently, concerning your abuse. Reflect on and describe similar self-talk that is still present in your life.

3. List specific fears you have now or have had in the past as a result of your sexual abuse.

4. Describe ways in which you have tried to compensate for your fears. What sinful strategies, if any, have you used to deal with your fears? Have they worked in overcoming any of your fears?

5. Write a detailed summary describing events that caused you to feel the most lonely or abandoned as a child, as a teenager, and as an adult.

6. Describe how it felt to be emotionally, verbally, and/or physically abandoned as a result of your sexual abuse. Make a list of all the people that abandoned you.

7. Tell how you have tried to compensate in your own life for the loneliness you have experienced.

8. In a separate notebook, keep a journal for one week of what happens when you use James 4:7 ("So be subject to God—stand firm against the devil; resist him and he will flee from you") in dealing with fear and loneliness.

9. Read all of chapter 13 of Paul's First Letter to the Corinthians, replacing the word *love* with *God*. Does this change any feelings you have toward God? If so, please explain.

10. Tell what Matthew 11:28–30, quoted here from the *New American Standard Bible*, means to you and your relationship with God.

   "Come to Me, all who are weary and heavy-laden, and I will give you rest. Take My yoke upon you, and learn from Me, for I am gentle and humble in heart; and you shall find rest for your souls. For My yoke is easy, and My load is light."

11.

Overcoming the Darkness—
Issues of Trust and Control

For thou art my lamp, O Lord: and the Lord will lighten
my darkness. . . . As for God, His way is perfect; the
word of the Lord is tried; he is a buckler to all them that
trust in him.

—2 Samuel 23:29, 31, KJV

Late one night, as I was sitting in a restaurant, I ordered
decaffeinated tea because I didn't want any caffeine in it
to keep me awake. When the tea came, I checked the tea bag
to make certain that the tea was decaffeinated. There was no
label. Immediately I became suspicious and called the wait-
ress to the table. I asked her to confirm that I was truly
drinking decaffeinated tea. She quickly answered in the
affirmative. I pointed out to her that there was no label
stating that the tea was decaffeinated. We exchanged a few
more words of doubts and assurances. She left the table.
Throughout drinking the entire pot of tea, I kept wondering
if this truly was decaffeinated tea.

This story is really not of earth-shattering importance, but
it demonstrates the pervasiveness of the suspicion that is
often embedded in the minds of abuse victims. In those
individuals, trust has been shattered by the absence of safety.
Somewhere along the road of life all of us were meant to have
trust firmly established in our minds and in our hearts by
parents and other significant individuals. The victims of

abuse, especially of childhood incest, have had the very core of trust plucked from their psyches. They have a very difficult road ahead to regain the God-given ability to trust that should have been their birthright. Children who have been abused by a non-family member and who have healthy, nurturing families can somewhat more quickly respond to the right intervention. Victims who come from unstable and unreliable families face a greater challenge in developing the ability and faith to trust.

A Primary Meaning of Trust

The word *trust* has at least seven possible meanings, each in direct opposition to the action that takes place in sexual abuse. One of the Hebrew words for *trust* has the meaning "to support, to stay, and to be faithful." Our standard English dictionaries list as a primary definition of *trust* "to rely upon or place confidence in someone or something."

Victims of incest experience the exact opposite of these meanings from the perpetrator. A young woman who came to me for counseling described her childhood situation: "In one way it was always the same with my father—we never knew what was going to happen. Dad could be four different people in one night. I can remember, when I was three or four years old, sitting in a corner after he blew up, wondering what I had done. I couldn't figure it out. It seemed to me that every time this happened, it was because I didn't do something that I was supposed to do. However, as I got older, I knew it was because he was drunk! At any rate, all during those early years I would play a game in my head called 'Something Bad Is Going to Happen.' It made me feel better to remember that. That way I wouldn't hurt so bad when the inevitable happened. I would just tell myself, *Stupid, what did you expect? You knew it was going to happen.*"

Every victim develops some system by which to survive the lack of support and betrayal of confidence, whether this be physical, mental, or spiritual. We readjust in order to survive the chaos in which we live. We have already noted that trust is a God-given ability, to be learned by humans from humans through parental nurturing and stability. Sexual abuse, especially from within the family, destroys the ability to trust. A dysfunctional family system also destroys that ability.

Trust as Hope and Expectation

One of the most precious definitions of *trust* listed in our dictionaries is "to place hope in someone or something; to expect confidently." Victims learn only too well not to have hope in or confident expectation of someone. They learn to survive, usually alone. Many victims believe that people in general are instruments of cruelty. Holding this belief, victims make certain that they avoid people. The problem, of course, is that God created us not to be alone but to be in communion with other humans and with Him. Without the ability to trust, the ability to risk—to allow oneself to be vulnerable—is lost. Many victims can't even trust themselves.

It is a terrible tragedy to live a life without security and to be in constant fear. Once a victim grows to adulthood, danger is, for the most part, not to be anticipated on a daily basis, but the fear and the insecurities evoked by the perpetrators are still present. The adult victim is often without security, without hope, and without confidence. Because of living in fear, trust is impossible.

Jeanie explains, "Growing up, I knew I couldn't trust anyone. My mother was off doing her own thing, and who knows where my father was. And with the step-dads, uncles, and brothers, you name it; I could trust them for one thing— they were going take what they wanted. The only good thing was that I knew one day I would grow up. What I didn't know, though, was that for close relationships I would pick every lousy person that was out there. No one was there for me growing up and no one was there for me afterwards. I've married three times. They were all bums. One even molested my kid.

"I really wanted my life to be different, to be better. I know there are good people out there. I've seem them at church, though sometimes I even wonder about them. But there must be someone that is good.

"I know I haven't been perfect, and I have a lot wrong with me, but I really can't believe all this badness. I don't know why I keep getting with the wrong guys. It's like I have a great big sign on my head that says, 'Hey! Come abuse me!' I don't even worry any more about whether I can trust them or not; I know I can't trust my own head, so I just don't get involved.

"There is one thing I have learned—to trust money. All I think about now is putting money in the bank. I do put some away every week, but it doesn't seem to add up too fast."

Trust as Shelter and Refuge

Another definition of *trust* likens it to "taking shelter in a safe place." But with abuse, victims learn that there is no place to flee to. Unfortunately, too many never learn that you can flee to God. Instead, the world they know teaches that you must survive by yourself and that no one is there for you. You are alone, and not secure. Perhaps this is the case with you, the reader of this book—that you don't trust anyone, not yourself, not even God. Then the greatest tragedy for you will be that you are rejecting the very One who can save you from the effects of your abuse. He is the One who can teach you to trust the right people. He is your refuge—the place to flee to.

Libby says she cried every day of her childhood that she can remember, and every day she asked God to let her die. She begged Him to help, to rescue her from her horror. She even prayed that her daddy would die. She prayed every kind of prayer she could think of for God's help. "So why then," she asked me, "should I believe God cares when I pray now?" I couldn't give her an overwhelming answer that would light up the sky with fireworks; I could only give the answer that we must never stop trying until we succeed. The only time we truly fail is when we stop trying.

No matter how it looks to you as you are suffering from the deceptions of abuse, God is and was there with you in the abuse. He is also there for your recovery. The issue of trust is one that not only affects the victim personally, but also every person the victim encounters. Trust affects every relationship—relationship with God, relationship with spouse and family, even casual relationships. The need to be able to trust is at the very core of our existence. We were created as beings who have the choice as to whom or what we believe and whom or what we trust.

The Problem of Control

Sexual abuse distorts our understanding. As we try to compensate for an inability to trust and to feel secure, without fear, we tend to isolate, rationalize, avoid, run away; we attempt to check everything out, and we suspect all others. Mainly, we decide *we* can control our lives. Even when the control fails, we keep on trying to control. We set conditions and expectations for all relationships, including our relationship with God, in order not to risk trusting. The problem, of course, is that we are miserable. We are not in control, but we are in fear.

Sometimes we believe that if we let down even for a moment someone will find out that we can be easily hurt. Any sign of weakness or vulnerability is unthinkable. If others discover we are weak, they will have power over us and this knowledge will be used against us. But there is a haven to which we can go and learn again to trust. Christian counseling provides just such a place—a safe environment where individuals can be loved for who they are. In my work with groups I hear victims say again and again that the only place they feel safe is when they come to the group. And eventually, as the Lord continues to work in their lives, victims begin to feel safe in other places and with other people.

A Fragile Flower

If you are a victim of abuse, you are like a fragile flower that life has attempted to destroy by one storm after another. Even if you have developed a hard heart because of your abuse, you are still that fragile flower that is being blown apart. It is never too late to get out of the storm and into an atmosphere of regeneration.

Martha couldn't hug anyone when she first came to group. She kept her distance by pushing her chair to the outside of the circle and only sharing occasionally. It was easy for me to see how much she hurt, and I prayed that she would let go of the pain. After several sessions she gradually revealed the trauma of abuse by her brother, the guilt of three abortions, and the present misery of living with an abusive husband. Letting go of her emotions, she began to allow herself the freedom to cry, to forgive, to love again. As she gave the control to God and took steps to trust in Him, she cried very deeply and for a very, very long time.

Now she hugs a little and smiles a lot more, and she believes in herself. She always trusted God for her salvation, but now she trusts Him for her refuge. When she stopped trying to control everyone and everything in her life, she realized that for the first time in her life she was no longer being controlled. She was free—free to make choices she had always wanted to make, free to love, free enough to trust someone to really love her.

Learning True Control

Every victim of abuse, to one degree or another, must deal with the issue of control. Because we had absolutely no control in our lives over sexual abuse, we are tempted to feel that if we are in control now, we will no longer be abused. Almost certainly, the more we attempt to control, the more we will be controlled. The more we attempt to control our circumstances, the more our circumstances will control us.

It is important also to realize that as long as we attempt to control, we will never really attempt to trust. In other words, if we can control circumstances, then we really have eliminated the need to trust. Of course, as we already know, we can't control our circumstances; consequently we end up confused and broken. Some people, for a period of time, are successful at controlling their environment, but eventually this fails because it is impossible to sustain. It takes a great deal of energy to manipulate and control our environment. To deny the pain of abuse takes still more energy. These exhausting painful and negative emotions, pushed down, will eventually emerge as physical problems (psychosomatic illness), emotional problems (depression or anxiety), or behavioral problems (destructive behavior, last-straw reactions).

Victims attempt many ways of readjusting to their lack of security and dealing with their fear, but learning to trust is the road to recovery. When I learned to trust God fully, no matter what the circumstances were, I knew that I was a long way down the road in my own recovery. At first, I attempted to trust God in small areas and at the same time, to learn to trust myself. I don't know exactly when it happened, but finally one day when the circumstances were such that it seemed God was too late to help, I somehow still knew that He would get me through this ordeal. Until this point in my life, I thought I was in control; I thought I had trusted God completely and that I was a great woman of faith. Suddenly I realized that control blocks faith.

Now I try to trust God completely—even when I see things happening that I don't like. I've learned and am continuing to learn to trust people. I have learned that some people can be trusted only for certain things and others can be trusted more completely. I don't need to control them. I don't need to keep people at a distance. I do admit and know that I need people, and that is good and not bad. In fact, God made us all to need each other—it is not good to be alone.

Scott, a good-looking, well-built man in his forties, describes giving up his control. "Being in control was easy for me, since I was a man and I was supposed to be in control. I controlled my wife and my son and daughter. My wife was an abuse victim, so it was easy to dominate her. My daughter ran away and got pregnant, but I never let up keeping my thumb pressed hard on her every move. They told me at work that they wanted to promote me, but I couldn't let go. They said I didn't know how to delegate. My son seemed to be the only one that was not affected by all this. I hope that's true. At least it seems that way now. He is a good person; he always does the right thing.

"Finally I lost it—my control over myself. I cried and cried. I was an abuse victim too, and I hated my abuser and I hated myself for living the lies that I had lived all my life. I told my wife first. For years we'd had sex problems—she had heavy guilt feelings over her own abuse, so I had just been letting that be the issue. But at this point, we were in separate bedrooms and I didn't have any desire for sex. I still don't.

"Over the years, I tried it all, every form of sex, but for a long time now I haven't wanted any sex at all. I never had any desire for my daughter, but sometimes I'd want my son. Thank God I never did anything to him. I did control them all in every other way. I determined when we ate, what we ate, where we went, and what we did. I'm exhausted and so is my family. I know the abuse is not the only issue in my life, but it is a deep seed within me, and I really want to be free from the torment."

Nonproductive Attempts to Control

It is typical behavior for victims to attempt to control their circumstances in every way they can. We've already looked at several—such things as isolation, money, and people. There are many more, and we will examine some of them. The challenge, more than itemizing the possibilities, is to discover what areas each of us is trying to dominate in our own lives. It's often difficult to recognize the clues, especially if the area of control is an integral part of the victim's personality or job responsibility. For instance, if you are very rigid in your daily life, you may think that you are only neat or timely rather than that you are controlling others by forcing them to do everything a certain way at a certain time and so on. You can even feel a real sense of peace because everything went the way it was supposed to.

Claire describes Christmas. "The abuse was always worse at Christmas. My dad was home more, and he got drunker. Anyway, I was sure when I grew up that I was going to make things right. Christmas was going to be special and perfect, no matter what. When I had my own home, I saw to it that we had all the decorations and everything else ready way ahead of time, even a train under the tree. But I always overspent. I definitely yelled too much at my kids because they didn't want to do things just my way. If anyone was late on Christmas day, I totally blew up. I was awful. I feel better now that I don't feel compelled to have this perfect Christmas. Actually, I feel relieved. I do feel empty, though."

Claire is only now at the point in her journey toward recovery where she is learning to let go. She is pretty typical of victims who try to control their circumstances by making everything perfect, in keeping with certain expectations of which others may be unaware. Unfortunately, the method by which Claire attempts to demonstrate this control is through her anger, also a typical pattern among victims. Claire is prone to sudden outbursts of anger and violent overreaction to any deviations from her rigid standards. Her task now is to learn not to suppress her pain and hurt, the root cause for her need to control, but to express it appropriately. She is learning to deal with her anger.

Claire has announced that this next Christmas she is going to ask people what special thing they want to do for that day. She plans not to overspend and not to worry at all about everything being perfect. She prays earnestly every day that her anger is no longer a weapon that she uses to control her environment. Claire is doing well and can even laugh about her own rigidity. She says, "I know I am trying to control when I get angry inside because someone didn't do something just the way I wanted."

Jeralyn's method of controlling others is by making them feel guilty. She does so much for everyone else that they usually do what she wants just because she is so good to them. But, as Jeralyn admits, "The truth is that I am the one who feels guilty all the time. In fact, I see that I really don't control them as much as they control me. The slightest suggestion that I don't love them or don't want to help them sends me on a guilt trip. Then I would do anything to prove my love and my concern, and unfortunately I usually do. Then I get angry. I don't ever really feel in control."

Steps to Trust and Discernment

So far in this chapter, I've tried to show why, as a victim of abuse, you will want to deal with the issue of how you control as well as how others control you. You will also want to know when to trust and when to distrust. Often victims are all-or-nothing individuals, making it difficult for them to take even small steps in the area of trust. After meeting individuals whom we've immediately trusted, only to find ourselves revictimized in one way or another, or, conversely, having failed to recognize trustworthy persons who would have helped us, we know that we must develop a healthy awareness for the appropriate placement of our trust.

The best place to start with trust, obviously, is with God. This is a process that includes praying and listening for and recognizing answers to our prayers. It also includes reading and studying the Word and hearing the understood Word of God through his servants and ministers. As a beginning, we can cry out for God and say we believe in Him. And we will probably find that we do believe at a certain level. God will be faithful, and our trust and confidence will be rewarded as we are able to give Him the control of our lives. (Try it; I did, and I know it works.)

Each of us, victim or not, learns to trust God at some point in our life's journey. Even individuals from wonderful, nurturing family systems are challenged in their ability to trust God when afflictions of the world come upon them. Give yourself time. Most of all, give God time.

Your trust in yourself will grow as you are better able to trust God, to place your confidence in Him, to have hope in Him, and to live in freedom from fear, protected by His power. Knowing when to trust or distrust is a gift from God called discernment. Hebrews 5:14 culminates in a passage exhorting us to learn and practice the teachings of God so that our senses have been "exercised to discern both good and evil." Clearly it is not God's desire for any one of us to trust the wicked and distrust the faithful.

Since, as victims, we have suffered clouded vision as a result of having been abused, it is very important for us to pray for the ability to discern. In fact, I believe it is a prayer for all of us to pray for the rest of our lives. We need to be able to recognize good and evil and to see the results of both. We need to hear the truth and to sense deception. We also need the experience of being in a group or counseling situation where openness and trust is modeled. Pray for discernment so you can engage in healing and helpful relationships.

There is no smooth road that I or anyone can pave for you, but I hope you have become convinced that readjusting to your abuse by attempting to control your world will only lead to disaster. A life without trust is a life without freedom—a life in bondage to every area you have chosen to control. It is a life without security and full of fear. Pray a simple prayer to God and give Him the control of your life. Even though you won't yet know all that the prayer will mean, and though you may often take the control back from God, pray the prayer.

You already know that I was very angry at God in the beginning, but since I could do nothing, that anger gave way to helplessness. I had no choice but to try to trust God; I had used all my other options. I had even tried all the ways that usually kept me in control. Nothing worked. He was all that was left. And He was there, as always, faithful and secure.

Waiting in Trust

This chapter would not be complete without one last definition for *trust* : "to expect confidently; to wait." It seems I had waited all my life and I hated to realize that I still had to wait. But to trust is to do what God expects of you, and many times He requires waiting. It's been a long road, a well-traveled road, but a powerful road.

There will be a day, even when you sin, even when you are betrayed, even when you feel God is too late, that you will be like the psalmist who wrote these words:

> For the Lord has not despised nor abhorred the
>   affliction of the afflicted;
> Neither has He hidden His face from him;
> But when he cried to Him for help, He heard.
> (Psalm 22:24, KJV)

The psalmist cast himself upon God and God delivered him. The psalmist knew God loved him. Trust God and let Him deliver you from all your fears, all your needs to control. Let Him set you free. Let Him teach you to trust that which is trustworthy.

WORKBOOK

1. Who or what have you trusted in to protect yourself from the pain of your abuse? Why did you choose to place your trust with these persons or things? Have they fulfilled your expectations?

2. Explain how it felt to take the risk in trusting the persons or things you named in your answer to the first question. Describe an area of risk with which you are still struggling.

3. List and describe areas of your life where you feel secure.

4. What fears are you aware of that keep you from truly trusting people and God? What is the worst thing that could happen if you trusted someone? The best thing?

5. What do you notice about people when you try to determine whether they "measure up"?

6. Describe how you control others in your life and how you are controlled by others.

7. What specific behavior that maintains your control would you like to change in your life?

8. Evaluate your own ability to be trusting and to be distrusting of people and situations in your life.

9. Tell what Psalm 22:24 (quoted near the end of p. 153) can and does mean to you.

10. Write a brief letter to God describing your fears in trusting Him. What is one thing you could do today to help build a bridge of trust between you and God?

12.

Forgetting the Darkness—
The Process of Forgiveness

Do not rejoice over me, O my enemy.
Though I fall I will rise;
Though I dwell in darkness, the Lord is
      a light for me.
                    —Micah 7:8, NASB

With each chapter I start, my impulse is to say that it is the most important in the book, and each one *is* extremely important to your recovery. But without being capable of forgiveness—the focus of this chapter—you cannot walk in the wholeness God has for you.

If you are reading through this book very rapidly, and have not yet had time to process all the difficult pain of your abuse, the very mention of forgiveness will seem unthinkable. The anger it may raise in you is very natural and to be expected, for you have not walked far enough down the path to feel otherwise. Perhaps you still need to express unreleased anger. Perhaps you have not come out of denial in an area of pain. Perhaps you believe if you forgive, the perpetrator is forgiven and no longer accountable to God for the sin.

Wherever you are in your journey toward recovery, please try to read this chapter. Just because it is talking about forgiveness doesn't mean that I am handing you a mandate from God that says you *must* forgive your offender this very instant! You don't have to. You can forgive when you are ready. A negative reaction only indicates that God's further help may be needed in whatever area you are still hurting. So, as you read, please remember that this chapter is simply the presentation of His principles of forgiveness, and it will only be through Him that you may eventually be motivated to take this step.

In chapter 5, we looked in depth at the story of Joseph as it illustrated the principles of God's restoration, but very little was said about forgiving and forgetting. Now let's study that topic in this chapter.

Why Can't We Forgive?

First let's consider the reasons why we may not want to forgive.

We may be too angry, we may be too hurt or we may be too afraid. We sometimes choose not to forgive because we have a false belief that unforgiveness will protect us from being hurt again. Inevitably the opposite occurs, and the offense continues to affect us as the pain turns into rage and bitterness.

Joyce, in group, says over and over, "I am not going to forgive that ——. He doesn't deserve it. Anyway, it was all I had to hold onto every time he came near me. I would say, 'I am never going to forgive him for this.' If I forgive him it would be like he won. He wasn't going to win then, now, or ever. I will not let go. I won't forgive him. It's like saying what he did was okay."

Another misconception about forgiveness is that granting it somehow gives the person who has wronged you permission to hurt you again. Forgiving someone does *not* give that person *permission* to hurt you again, even if that does happen. In most family situations we can recognize forgiveness (for many hurts, not just sexual abuse) as a healthy part of the relationship, and that includes the probability of being hurt again by the same family members. But with sexual abuse, the crime is so vicious that we grasp for any way, appropriate or not, to handle the pain. Unforgiveness seems a way to handle the pain of the abuse.

Who Is Hurt by Unforgiveness?

We believe unforgiveness will somehow hurt the perpetrator, but the opposite is true. Perpetrators, unforgiven, go right on doing what they want to do. They never considered us in the first place, and our unforgiveness has absolutely no effect on their behavior. However, it does have a great impact on our lives.

Both the Greek and the Hebrew verbs for *forgive* may also be translated "to send away." For the victim it could mean to send away the hurt, the anger, the bitterness, the sadness, and, most important, the abuse. Jesus, not you or I, is the One who died on the cross for the forgiveness of sin, even if we do feel as if we have been crucified. At some point, we must recognize that the forgiveness we may grant is really for us. Our unforgiveness holds us in bondage to the pain of the abuse. Certainly our forgiving of the perpetrator affects our responses and relationship to him or her, but the perpetrator is not wholly forgiven unless he or she goes before God and seeks *His* forgiveness. God is the One who takes the sin of the world away. He is the one who atoned for the sin. Most important, God is the one, and the only one, who pardons the sin of sexual abuse.

In the Old Testament, the Hebrew word for *pardon* is only used in connection with God and implies forgiveness by God when God is offended. Certainly humans sin against humans, but sin is also against God. Sexual abuse is a sin against God and must be pardoned by God as all other sin is pardoned by Him.

Angie expressed her feelings by saying, "I don't want my abuser to be forgiven. If I forgive him, it will be like he gets off. Like he gets off scot free. I hate that. Why should he get off? All he has to do is say, 'I'm sorry,' and he's forgiven. Baloney!

I just hate the whole idea. It makes me sick to even think about it. I want him to be punished for what he did to me. I've been punished for forty-seven years."

As Angie demonstrates so well, forgiveness confronts the victim with a difficult challenge, but unforgiveness will create a multitude of problems for the victim. Grasping unforgiveness as a way of life forces one to bear again and again the offenses of the sexual abuse. George, who refuses to forgive his uncle, constantly relives in his mind the torment of the sexual abuse. We must understand that when we don't forgive and allow God to restore His love to us, we risk walking in bitterness and despair as we feel the force of unforgiveness through stress, turmoil, and horrible memories.

When the Offense Is Too Great

In *The Search For Significance,* author Robert McGee states several reasons individuals do not forgive, one of which is that the offense is too great. About 75 percent of my clients have been sexually, physically, and/or emotionally abused, and they give me reason to support McGee's statement. But despite the great offense of sexual abuse, for our own complete recovery we must let go of it and of the offender. It harms only us to refuse to forgive the perpetrator, the co-perpetrator, and anyone or anything else that would impede us from our goal.

From the devastating betrayal of a child to the outrage of a violent rape, the offenses *are* too great, but God is willing to pardon all sin for those who repent and believe. We victims let go of the affliction that results from the sin by forgiving. Joseph had to make the same decision on his long journey to Egypt. He pleaded and begged his brothers to lift him out of the pit, but they refused and sold him to the Ishmaelites.

Joseph's life journey must surely have included issues of forgiveness. Perhaps he needed to forgive Potiphar (his

Egyptian master), his brothers, and even his father for not preparing him more and for favoring him above his brothers. Perhaps he needed to forgive himself for acting so pridefully about his dreams. I am sure Joseph thought long, hard, and prayerfully over his plight and at some point let go of all his hurt, anger, fear, and pride. He let go and forgave.

The Importance of an Apology

Another prime reason we may find it difficult to forgive is that the abuser never said he or she was sorry. Linda confronted her father, expecting him to say how sorry he was. She really wanted to forgive him; all he needed to say to her was that he was sorry. But his only response was that he didn't ever remember doing anything to her. The anger burned deep within Linda. It was as if she had been abused all over again. Finally she was able sorrowfully to shed tears over his denial. Later, in my office, she wept deeply for close to an hour and afterwards seemed less angry in general. Eventually she forgave her father. She tells me now that she feels happier than she has in years, although there is a part of her that still grieves about a father-daughter relationship that could only be based on her father's denial, not his repentance.

Forgiveness and Restoration

While Linda's forgiveness did not restore a relationship with her father, it restored her: "I have a peace, a reality, a maturity about life that I never had before. I don't stay around my dad looking for that word or glance that will tell me how sorry he is. I feel peaceful and joyful about who I am and I have objectivity about who he is. Now, I love me. I don't have to look for love from him because what he doesn't give, my Father in Heaven gives me."

Some victims find it difficult to forgive because the perpetrator committed the abuse deliberately and repeatedly. Here the problem for the victim is in trying to make sense of the abuse. If it had been without forethought or deliberation, forgiveness might have seemed easier. Yet, if we were to base our forgiveness on forgiving only accidental sin, we probably wouldn't be able to forgive very much.

It is a fact that most perpetrators, when confronted, deny any abuse. Most perpetrators argue in some unhealthy manner that what they did was the victim's fault, that the experience was a good one for the victim, or that the victim really wanted it. But forgiveness and restoration is not a one-time event for the victim. The first forgiving word spoken to God about the perpetrator generally and biblically begins the process of healing from the destructive effects of the abuse. However, the victim will probably forgive and pray the prayer of restoration many times before feeling whole again.

Recognizing Rationalization

Some victims don't forgive the perpetrators, they rationalize; that is, in the process of forgiving they continue to deny their own feelings and thus offer the perpetrator cheap grace. Some may spiritually rationalize by saying, "I must forgive my abuser because I am a child of God." Some find an excuse for the offender, saying such things as "he (or she) had a really bad childhood," or "I feel really sorry for him (her), since I found out about his (her) life." The problem with this logic is that it is rationalization, not forgiveness. I, too, would feel very sorry for someone whose early years had been marred by bad circumstances, but a tragic childhood doesn't give that person permission to rape or commit any other sin. Many thousands of people with such childhoods choose to find a more productive way to live their lives than sexually abusing someone.

Victims are particularly prone to rationalize about the co-perpetrator's role. Tammy explains: "I just don't feel I have to forgive my mother. She didn't know what was going on. Yes, she was in the house sometimes, but she was always in the other room. She had so many problems of her own to deal with that truly she just didn't have time. I had five younger brothers and sisters. She had to work part-time. I am surprised that she didn't run away from it all. When she found out, she was brokenhearted. She told me she had been abused as a child herself.

"It's true that when the abuse would happen I would wonder why she didn't do something to help me. I would sometimes think that she surely must know what was going on. Sometimes I would cry and think she just didn't care enough about me to see anything."

Tammy did finally forgive her mother also for the co-perpetration. It was important for Tammy, as well as for each victim, to see that regardless of how innocent the co-perpetrator is, he or she still needs to be forgiven. That old fragment in the memory of the victim needs to be reborn with the freedom of forgiveness.

Tammy's mother sat with me in a session crying. "I knew something wasn't right. I would feel uncomfortable. It was as if God was telling me, but I would say to myself, 'Don't be foolish.' I just ignored it."

Special Problems of Codependency

Another major area of recovery for the victim which is affected by the ability to forgive is codependency. In the circumstances of her sexual abuse, Tammy is a codependent and, as such, is displaying a typical lack of objectivity and feeling of over-responsibility for the abuse. Consequently she is truly unable to implement the principle of forgiveness. The codependent victim may not feel free to forgive because of the role reversal, in which she has exchanged places with the co-perpetrator and is thus not the victim. Additionally, this same codependent victim may think it unnecessary to forgive because of being partly responsible (in her exchanged role) for the abuse. For a detailed discussion of the pitfalls to codependent behavior, see Pat Springle's book *Codependency*.*

When You Forgive All Perpetrators

You may expect that, at some point in your journey toward recovery, God will make you aware of the importance of forgiving all perpetrators. In Joseph's life journey, he had many individuals whom he could forgive. He did that, and we saw earlier that God restored him to the position of second in command to the Pharaoh in Egypt. We also noted that Joseph and the wife given to him by the Pharaoh had a child whose name, Manasseh, translates into English as "causing to forget."

What a miracle there truly is for every believer who chooses to participate in God's forgiveness. Many, or perhaps most, victims, believe they can at some point forgive, but they don't believe they can forget. In fact, we hear that statement, "I forgive, but I can't forget," so often that we want to shut it off. But God *can* cause our pain to be forgotten through His restoration.

Forgiving Is Our Decision

For me and for every victim, to forgive is a decision we will have to make. I wasn't so overwhelmed with love nor did I become so spiritual that I just found myself forgiving everyone. I *decided* to forgive. I prayed for restoration and God truly caused the pain to be forgotten. It also was not a one-time event, even though I believe that the first time I forgave met all the scriptural requirements. Typically, the process is one that does require a long period of time.

---

*Codependency: A Christian Perspective, 2d ed. (Houston and Dallas, TX: Rapha Publishing/Word, Inc., 1990).

I was in touch with the obvious effects my abuse had had upon me, and I implemented the principle of forgiveness in every area I understood. I forgave the perpetrators. I forgave the co-perpetrators. I forgave the betrayal of my innocence. I forgave the thieves of my childhood. I forgave the shattering of my identity. I forgave everything I could think of. I began to feel better and less angry, but still empty.

Then I started forgiving the perpetrator for each flashback that still tormented my heart and my mind. Every time a memory of abuse would burst across my mind, I would forgive the perpetrator. I would ask God to restore His love to me in place of the despair that had come from human sin. Every time I overreacted and became too angry, I would ask God to forgive me for that sin. I would ask Him to replace with His love what had been taken from me. It took about fifteen months for me to process all my forgiving. Even when I didn't want to forgive, I would do it anyway. I was determined to do everything I could to believe in God. If He could really restore me, I knew somehow that I could make it through life.

Eventually people began to notice an inner change. One friend said to me, "Cindy, what happened to you? You're not as angry." I couldn't explain to her at that time. I just smiled and said, "God has happened to me." I could intellectually remember the abuse, but God had caused me to forget the pain of it. I didn't feel dirty, used, or anything negative. I felt full of life and hope. Of course, my worth, my confidence, my identity were not all restored, and I wasn't sure who I was or who I was supposed to be, but I was on the right road.

Sometimes I would meditate and ponder things in my heart. I still felt anxious, but not as anxious. I still had self-doubt, but not as often. I realized God had given His love to me and caused the pain to leave, but it seemed clear that He had still more for me to learn. He wanted me to find my significance for Him. He wanted me to find a new joy in relating to others. He wanted abundant life for me, not merely survival.

Recovery is between us and God. Yet God does not offer us the option of unforgiveness. In the Lord's Prayer, we are taught to pray to God to "forgive us our debts as we forgive our debtors." Each day, I still pray the prayer of forgiveness and restoration. If someone sins against me or if I sin, something has been lost to me. Sin takes and God gives. God gives restoration as a by-product of forgiveness.

Don't be dismayed at this point. If you're not ready to forgive, God will help you to get there. If you can make a decision to forgive and if you can trust what God says even just a little, He will restore you.

A woman in my group yelled at me, "Cindy, if you are lying to me I am going to want to kill you." I assured her I was not lying to her, not because of what I have said, but rather because of what God has said. God will restore all the love that has been stolen.

Forgive. Send away all the hurt, the bitterness, the pain, the anger, and the abuse. Allow God to replace the despair, the loneliness, and the betrayal with His love, His joy, and His blessings.

WORKBOOK

1. Make a list of those you need to forgive, including perpetrators, co-perpetrators, yourself, and even God. Choose to forgive them. Ask God to help you forgive them and to show you the pathway of forgiveness.

2. Tell what you think forgiving can mean in your life. What can you do to prepare for this process?

3. What do you need to have restored to your life? What have been your greatest losses?

4. What incidents or memories would you most like to forget?

5. How have you used unforgiveness in your life as a means of ridding yourself of the pain caused by your abuse? How has it helped or hindered you?

6. Joel 2:25–26, Nahum 2:2, and 1 Peter 5:10 speak of restoration. What does God say in those verses about restoration and what it can mean in your life?

7. Read Psalm 23 again. What can God restore in your identity? What path do you think you need to follow?

8. What do you need to send away from your life with the principle of forgiveness?

9. After one week of forgiving as many individuals who have harmed or angered you as you can, describe any differences that you feel in your life.

10. Micah 7:8 is found in the heading of this chapter. How do you relate to this scripture? What can or does it mean in your life?

13.

Destroying the Darkness—
Intimacy in Relationships

Then watch out that the light in you may not be
darkness. If therefore your whole body is full of light,
with no dark part in it, it shall be wholly illuminated
as when the lamp illumines you with its rays.
—Luke 11:35–36, NASB

W hen it came time to name this chapter on intimacy, I felt
really moved of God to call it "Destroying the Darkness." I believe that when victims acquire the ability to be
intimate, the evil darkness that has come upon them is
destroyed. As Luke says in the scripture that heads this
chapter, when the dark part of you is gone, you will be wholly
illuminated.

At the start of recovery from sexual abuse, most victims are
unable to have any real intimacy with people, as they still are
in the darkness of their trauma. With God's help that darkness will be made into light. My intention in this chapter is not
only to help you identify what intimacy is and what it is not
but also to take the great leap into a deep intimacy with God.

Barriers to Intimacy

We have already discussed many of the potential barriers
to achieving intimacy such as betrayal, lack of trust, and fear.
As we know from chapter 3, "The Family in Darkness,"
victims are often violated by the very system that God sent

into the world to teach them the concept of intimacy. The abuse and the abuser, as well as the family situation, will be factors in determining the degree to which you, the victim, will be able to express intimacy.

Many victims decided years ago that they absolutely do not want any intimacy with anyone. Others crave intimacy and have tried many things to meet this aching need deep inside their souls. Whatever you have tried or have not tried, if you are unable to have real intimacy with people, there is still a darkness in your soul.

Embarking on the Journey

Wherever you are on the difficult voyage from isolation to intimacy, for your own happiness you must hold your course, or, if you have not yet begun that journey, equip yourself with God's chart and ready yourself to embark. God wants us not only to be close to Him, but to be close to others—our mates, children, families, and friends. All these relationships are affected by our inability to be intimate.

As you become free to experience deep intimacy, you will find that there are people in your life who will not be able to respond to your new openness. This is disappointing, of course, but in time, as your own increased understanding and empathy become apparent to them, improved relationships may result. In any case, their lack of participation in intimate relationships doesn't have to stop your growth in this area. Hopefully, your spouse, your children, and your family will be able to grasp intimacy along with you.

Victims struggle greatly with the issue of intimacy. God-given needs for intimacy are and were always there, but were never met in a healthy way or with any consistency. Every boundary of intimacy was violated by the sexual abuse. Victims are afraid of putting deep trust in anyone lest they may be betrayed again. They decline to take any initiative toward developing closer relationships of any kind or becoming deeply committed to anyone. However, most are too lonely and afraid to be independent from others. The dilemma is often overwhelming, as they hunger for this intimacy like an unfed child hungers for food.

The Nature of Intimacy

Webster's Dictionary defines *intimacy* as "belonging to one's deepest nature; marked by a very close association with someone else; friendship that is marked by warmness and a long association; a very personal and private association with another individual." All of us should, and probably do, long for this kind of relationship.

Throughout the Bible many examples of a deep warmth and closeness in relationships can be found. Paul continually admonishes new Christians to love each other, to be supportive of each other, and to share with each other. Jesus' mother, Mary, went to Elizabeth, her friend and relative, to share the news of her pregnancy and remained with her three months. David trusted Jonathan, the son of King Saul, even as King Saul pursued David.

But who desires intimacy with us more than Jesus? We are deeply loved by Jesus. We are fully pleasing and acceptable to Jesus, and He would do anything to help us—even die for us. There isn't anything that He does not know about us. He cares about every detail, even to the number of hairs on our head. There is absolutely no condemnation in Jesus—only love. This deep, loving intimacy is ours if only we can let Jesus shine that light into our soul.

The Need for Intimacy

In my story at the beginning of this book you learned that there was a time when I had to accept the fact that I was lonely and miserable in isolation. I needed God. I needed people. I needed love. I needed intimacy. Eventually I found that intimacy as I journeyed toward restoration and recovery. Luke 12:3 (NASB) says, "Therefore whatsoever ye have spoken in darkness shall be heard in the light; and that which ye have spoken in the ear in closets shall be proclaimed upon the housetops." I want to assure you that whatever you have spoken and cried in your moments of desperation, God will restore you with His love. Intimacy destroys the darkness. Whether the abuse is from the world or from the principalities of darkness, the ability to be intimate will destroy the trauma of the abuse.

What Intimacy Is Not

Most of us who have been victims are afraid of intimacy because we fear it will mean violation of our boundaries. Remember this; get it firmly fixed in your mind: *it will not.* Intimacy does not mean a blind trust with anyone. Intimacy does not mean isolation, physical or emotional. Intimacy does not mean betrayal. Intimacy does not mean agreeing with another person when you know that person is not right. Intimacy does not mean disclosing private or personal information when you do not want or wish to. Intimacy does not mean bondage; it does not mean abuse.

What Intimacy Offers

Intimacy is freedom. Intimacy is the ability to set and maintain boundaries. Intimacy is the ability to disclose personal and private matters when and if you choose. Intimacy allows for trusting those who are trustworthy and for forming long-term, meaningful relationships with others who desire intimacy as well. Intimacy is the ability to accept the fact that no one human being will be able to meet all your needs. Intimacy is the ability to risk, to take the initiative of truly giving of yourself and allowing someone to know you and to see all that you are and all that you are not. Intimacy is the ability to keep secrets, but not be a secret. Intimacy is the ability to give and receive love. Intimacy is the deepest commitment of love and the deepest expression of love.

Intimacy and Group Therapy

Having in mind at least some concept of intimacy, let's begin to navigate our individual routes to intimacy. Joining a sexual abuse group, if you are not already taking part in one, is a good place to start. Certainly you can learn intimacy outside a group, but the environment offered by a group provides a safe place for you to begin taking the risk of being more open. (Reminder: please keep in mind the cautions about group participation that have been given in previous chapters.)

Intimacy and Neglect

An area of sexual abuse that has a profound effect on the ability to achieve intimacy is that of neglect and abandonment. As I described some parts of my childhood, I was actually describing the effects upon me of those issues. One of my clients wrote a description which I have paraphrased here:

"Neglect . . . it is more painful than death. You are not allowed to live or to die. You are not allowed to join or to belong. You are alive—existing but not living. You know you are not acceptable. You stare at people and things from a distance—observing, listening, and hurting. You see the pain, but you can't scream, because it isn't safe. It is not safe to cry, to want, to dream, to feel, to ask, or to desire. This is being abandoned."

Each one of us who experiences or has experienced this kind of neglect will need to pray for restoration again and again until we feel safe. The more we can talk, write, and express our feelings with supportive people, the more we will be able to express our desires, our feelings, and our needs.

Intimacy is sharing the private and personal things of our lives, but it is also the ability to ask for our private and personal needs to be met.

Pray specifically for all areas of neglect, abandonment, and abuse that you know keep you from risking yourself in relationships. Victims who have been neglected have an especially difficult time dealing with the self-hate that occurs in sexual abuse. Many victims of all kinds of abuse despise themselves, and consequently find it very difficult to receive concern and affection from others. It is very difficult to believe that someone could really love you. I urge you to take a second major step and begin to believe in yourself. God believes in you.

Who You Are in Christ

An important part of Rapha's resource materials is a declaration* which I ask my clients to read once every morning and once every evening. It helps them understand who they really are in Christ. When I first came across this declaration a few years ago, I believed all of its statements except the one that said I was fully pleasing to God. I had the head knowledge, but not the heart knowledge, of the scriptures that undergird that statement. But as I began to read the declaration on a daily basis, I began to receive in my heart the idea that, *yes, I am fully pleasing to God.* Even in all the ways that I am not yet what I know I should be, I am pleasing to Him. You may find statements that are hard for you to believe, statements that are different from the one I couldn't accept. But, keep in mind that this entire declaration is based on the scriptures, and it may help you, as it did me, to read it as often as you can. Remember that God really did make you an original, one-of-a-kind, special person.

---

*Reprinted from the Search for Significance series materials with the permission of Rapha, Inc.

Declaration

Because of Christ's redemption,
I am a new creation of infinite worth.

I am deeply loved,
I am completely forgiven,
I am fully pleasing,
I am totally accepted by God.
I am absolutely complete in Christ.

When my performance
reflects my new identity in Christ,
that reflection is dynamically unique.

There has never been another person like me
in the history of mankind,
nor will there ever be.
God has made an original,
one of a kind, a special person.

The Scriptures

I am deeply loved.

By this the love of God was manifested in us, that God has
sent His only begotten son into the world so that we might
live through Him. In this is love, not that we loved God,
but that He loved us and sent His Son to be the propitiation
for our sins. Beloved, if God so loved us, we also ought to
love one another.

—1 John 4:9–11

I am fully pleasing.
Therefore having been justified by faith we have the peace
with God through our Lord Jesus Christ.

—Romans 5:1

I am totally acceptable & accepted.
And although you were formerly alienated and hostile in mind, engaged in evil deeds, yet He has now reconciled you in His fleshly body through death, in order to present you before Him holy and blameless and beyond reproach. . . .
—Colossians 1:21–22

I am a new creation—complete in Christ.
. . . and in Him you have been made complete, and He is the head over all rule and authority. . . .
—Colossians 2:10

The Inability to Be Intimate

Let's recap some of the causes for the inability to be intimate. Sexual abuse itself, of course, is the major cause, along with all the effects of the abuse. Review the following list of probable causes for emotional isolation, and pray for specific understanding of how any of these causes have had an impact on your ability to be intimate. How did you learn to shut down emotionally? How did you learn to isolate yourself emotionally? You will probably want to reread what we have said in previous chapters as you review the list. There may also be areas you need to deal with that are not on the list.

Probable Causes for Emotional Isolation

Sexual abuse	Shame
Poor self-image	Guilt
Family messages	Fear
Abandonment	Depression
Neglect	Inability to trust

Reasons for Inability to Form Successful Intimate Relationships

Persons who have been sexually abused may:
1) fear relationships but continually express a desire or need for them; often avoid taking risks due to fear of abandonment or rejection
2) send a double message of wanting others to show affection, and rejecting affection that is offered
3) search for some magical quality in another person that will make them feel complete/tend to become immobilized by romantic obsessions
4) take themselves too seriously and be unable to joke with others
5) use sex to feel validated and complete
6) be too critical of partners and of self and have unrealistic standards; may interpret simple misunderstandings in the relationship as betrayal
7) be suspicious and constantly test people in relationships
8) constantly seek intimacy with another person; may be desperate for closeness but unable to be intimate
9) have a strong need for male approval but unsatisfied by female approval
10) be drawn to people who are unavailable, or who reject and abuse others
11) become addicted to a person but be unable to meet healthy needs of sex, love, and affection
12) become involved with sex addicts
13) be independent in relationships, yet possessive of others, sometimes to the point of extreme jealousy
14) exhibit compulsive behavior—taking drugs, drinking, smoking, eating, spending money
15) receive love of another person but keep on looking for someone more desirable to love them

When Our Needs for Intimacy Are Not Met

As you consider the following discussion of how we react when our intimacy needs are not met, note the individual stories that illustrate some of the different tendencies listed in the chart on the opposite page.

Self-Pity

Now that we have begun to identify specifically the causes for our emotional isolation, let's discuss our negative reactions to not having our intimacy needs met. One that most of us don't like to admit to, but with which we all deal, is self-pity. We feel sorry for ourselves and even pout and display oversensitivity. We say again and again, "Why did this happen to me?" As I wrote earlier, it is valid to feel sorry about the abuse, but self-pity is a pit that we must crawl out of. Cry a good cry again and again, but pray to get past this stage. Self-pity will not help your recovery. It will not help you to be intimate. Self-pity will isolate you all the more.

Anger

Another reaction is anger. As we discussed in chapter 8, anger must be dealt with appropriately. It should not lead to resentment, bitterness, or retaliation, but to recovery. Anger not only becomes our reaction to the abuse we experienced, but it also becomes a barrier to intimacy. We must learn to get past the anger.

Julie described that fragment inside of her: "No one was ever reliable. No one ever did what they said they would. I finally worked through my anger about most of this when I realized how it was affecting my life. When my husband would forget to turn out the light, I would go into a rage. I felt I'd been betrayed and that he'd done it on purpose. I knew this wasn't true, of course, because he had other things on his mind and had just forgotten it.

"I always expected so much of my friends that if they told

me they'd do something and then didn't follow through, I would never want to see them again. I'd begin to withdraw from them and most of the time the relationships ended. I never allowed them any room to just be human. They had to be perfect in the relationship.

"I really don't know how my husband managed for so many years. Once I asked him to bring me a candy bar. He forgot. I went into an out-and-out rage. At the moment it seemed he didn't care for me at all and that everything he stood for was a lie."

After counseling, Julie began to realize that she must learn to see people in the whole relationship, not just for one incident. We found that this kind of angry behavior was a fragment of Julie's reaction to her betrayal as a child. It was still affecting all her relationships, and in order to overcome it, she was going to have to learn to see things in perspective and not to judge people based on one incident or on the past. To help Julie accomplish this goal, I asked her (as I often do with my clients) to write on a 3x5 card a statement to read every morning and every evening asking God to bring to her attention any inappropriate responses to other persons.

Hardness of Heart

Sometimes victims react by developing a hardness of heart, perhaps putting a shell around themselves or resorting to bullying others weaker than they. Please ask God to give you a tender heart: a hard heart will only increase your pain. Even though you are an adult now and it may seem better to continue to protect yourself from intimacy, the result will only be overwhelming loneliness. Your reading of this book and attempting recovery really says *I want help, I need people.* Take as long as you need to recover, but allow God to plow the fallow ground of your hard heart.

A Judgmental Attitude

A major reaction to not having our needs met is to be critical of others. Victims tend to be very critical of their spouses and of their children. Part of the reason is that we are constantly standing in judgment of others because of our obsession with finding out whether or not they are going to betray us. We test every aspect of the relationship, always hoping we won't be betrayed. Another reason is that we tend to set standards that are too high and unrealistic, thereby assuring that we do not have to get too close, because no one will be able to measure up to the standard. It helps us keep everyone at a distance; therefore we don't have to risk intimacy.

There are many more negative reactions to the rejection victims feel because of their abuse. All of these are a part of you that God must restore so that you will have the freedom really to love.

Perfectionism, False Compassion, Attention-Demanding Behavior

Typically, we do try to readjust to our lack of ability to be intimate. If this God-given need is not met in a healthy way, most of us will attempt to have it met in a dysfunctional way. For instance, we may try perfectionism, an extreme of setting standards too high, with the result mentioned just above. Another unfruitful way is to have false compassion for others, helping hurting people not for their sake but so that we can feel their pain. This may help in part to meet our own ache inside, but it will not work forever. Some people adopt pets which they can safely love and depend upon to be loyal to them.

Others readjust by demanding attention. Perhaps they act like clowns or show-offs, or adopt extreme dress or loud personalities in order to get attention. Unfortunately, this does not meet their intimacy needs, and it often leads to rejection.

Compulsive Behavior

Probably the most common method employed in the attempt to have intimacy needs met involves some type of compulsive behavior—eating, smoking, drinking, spending money, engaging in promiscuity, or any other type of destructive behavior. These individuals, who feel lonely and often are already depressed, attempt to compensate for their low sense of self-worth by engaging in some type of behavior that feels good. They do not see any other way to release the pain they feel. The pain always comes back.

Leslie shares her story: "I would begin to feel empty. I was already depressed, but now I really hurt inside. I didn't know what I could do to help myself. I just wanted the pain to go away, even if only for a little while. I would start eating, and it did feel good. Many times I would go shopping and overspend. At the time I would feel happy, but later I would hate myself. The only thing I really accomplished was to get fat and to get in debt. I hate it and I hate myself."

Others try accumulating material things as a way of meeting their needs. They may feel better temporarily, but satisfying material lust cannot fill the God-given need for close relationships. Some victims give in to sexual lust. They feel they must have someone there to hold, to sleep with, and to have sex with. They often will do anything to achieve this, but more often this leads to being revictimized or to sexual addictions.

Suppression of the Need for Intimacy

Another common readjustment is to suppress the need for intimacy. When we have run out of ways for having our needs fulfilled, we try to make ourselves believe that we can live without intimacy. But we soon find we cannot really get along without this God-given need, so we again try the old ways.

The Substitution of Fantasy

Sometimes our fantasies keep us from intimacy. One victim, describing her fantasies of being raped, admits that she does know that rape would not be like her fantasies; it would be horrible. Her fantasies are full of helplessness and full of joy and of being overwhelmed. As the rape ends, she has an orgasm. She describes feeling full of shame and guilt over the fantasy, but in counseling resists dealing with her sexual dysfunction in her marriage. She gets pleasure out of the fantasy, but she is afraid to become intimate and commit to her husband sexually. She has never had an orgasm with her husband. This victim, of course, is in recovery and, with a husband committed to supporting her therapy, it is likely that issues will be resolved.

Unforgiveness

The last tool to avoid intimacy which we will mention here is unforgiveness. A full chapter has already been devoted to this subject, and that discussion applies here also. Suffice it to say that unforgiveness as an issue of debate between counselor and counselee is often a normal part of recovery for victims. But at some point, victims must allow themselves the freedom forgiveness brings. This will lead to the need to be intimate, because this need has temporarily been filled with the power of unforgiveness. You may feel empty, but that will produce the energy you need to grow up in the Lord.

Intimacy in Marriage after Sexual Abuse

An area of intimacy that sexual abuse commonly destroys is that of sexual relations in a marriage. Often individuals confide that they never had a problem with sex until they got married. Some relate that they were sexually active before marriage and wonder if God is punishing them now in their marriage. I assure you and them, He is not. Marriage often appears to present the same problems for the victim as the abusive situation did, in that victims feel that they "have to" engage in sex. Consciously or unconsciously, they feel that their power of choice once again has been taken from them.

Many times victims have flashbacks while having sexual relations with their spouse. Other times spouses may do something similar to what the abuser did, and victims will be unable to respond. Sometimes, before starting in recovery,

victims have been spared the common problem of dysfunction in the sexual area of their marriage. But during the
recovery process, they may no longer desire to have sex with
their partners because of emerging painful memories. All of
these things are normal for victims and can be worked
through with two committed, Christian partners. The counseling professional may even advise the couple to abstain
from sex for a period of time, but be assured that recovery will
work.

Characteristic Attitudes and Responses
of Female Sexual Abuse Victims toward Sex

Unable to enjoy kissing
Guilt and dirty feelings after sex or about sex
Problems concerning boundaries in sex
Inability to tolerate own body
Dissociation from own body during sex
Feeling of worthlessness if unable to provide sex
Wearing of seductive dress or asexual clothing
Inability to look at a naked man/feeling of revulsion
Phobic avoidance of penises
Inability to tell whether or not men are "coming on"
Effort to make "it" (life) better with sex
Avoidance of sexual activity or use of words associated with
     sex
Compulsive sexual behavior
Sexual acting out
Lack of sexual desire
Exhibitionism/lack of modesty
Extreme modesty
Alternation between compulsive sexual behavior and lack of
     sex drive
Feeling of being caught during sex
Fear of letting go during sex/stopping self in arousal and
     enjoyment

Crying during or after sex
Need for darkness during sex
Feeling of being good only for sex; abandonment feared if
    victim refuses to participate in sex
Lack of sensitivity in breasts; victim shuts self down
Difficulty with or inability to achieve orgasm
Need to feel helpless during sex
Fantasizing of rape
Aversion to masturbation
Aversion to parts of one's own body
Pain in vaginal area during sex
Nervousness at being stimulated
Inability to have drug- or alcohol-free sex
Desire to make partner responsible for sex
Preoccupation with other concerns during sex
Eagerness for sex to be over
Feeling of having to perform during sex
Inability to ask to have sexual needs met
Anger during and after sex at having been exploited
Inability to look at oneself nude
Aversion to touching oneself
Inability to be playful during sex
View of self as sex object
Need for sex to be dirty

Certainly the most physically intimate thing each of us does with another person is to have sexual relations. We uncover our bodies and leave ourselves very vulnerable to another person. No one has to ponder too long to recognize the distortion that sexual abuse brings to this God-given act of marriage. But somehow, with God's help, we, as victims, must regain our dignity and learn to share our dignity with our mates.

With God's help victims and victims' spouses must learn how to plant the victim in healthy soil. Perhaps the couples must begin with holding hands until the victim feels safe.

Perhaps the couple must commit to only holding one another for a time.

Often victims need to know from their partners that they would be loved by them even if they never had sex.

The Special Problems of the Single Person

I have used many examples of married victims with children to reveal the challenges of destroying the darkness that prevents intimacy in relationships, but the challenge for the single person has some unique elements.

I deal with many single victims where the casualness of the abuse has already taken its toll. Often the single victim is quite alone, perhaps too fearful to have married or perhaps having been in a marriage that ended in divorce. For a victim who is alone, becoming skilled in intimacy may be a somewhat more difficult path than he or she wants to follow. Obviously, circumstances for practicing the principles that will lead to a successful relationship do not present themselves as easily as they do for the married victim who is presently in a relationship. Remaining single may seem easier or better because many aspects of intimacy, including affection and sex as well as conflict, can be totally avoided. On the other hand, the married victim may find it more difficult to learn to be intimate with oneself. The victim who is single may not have all the issues of intimacy triggered without a mate, but learning the principles of recovery will help the recovered victim accept the challenge as it occurs in a future relationship.

The important part is to learn the joy of intimacy and to destroy unhealthy isolation of self.

The following story of terror illustrates an experience that many women dread may happen to them some day. The single victim who related the story has been diagnosed with genital herpes and, far more devastating, must wait six months before AIDS testing can be expected to give dependable results. The rapists were caught, but wouldn't give the required consent to be tested.

"I am twenty-five years old, single and have a great job. Life should be at the top for me, but it isn't—not since a few weeks ago when I was awakened in the middle of the night because a pillow was stuffed into my face. I woke up dazed and tired, but my whole being was suddenly gripped with terror. Two young men, very mean and hard-looking, stood above me, glaring down and yelling obscene words.

"My roommate had gone away for the weekend. I was helpless. They blindfolded me and tied me up with cords and began doing all sorts of things to me . . . unspeakable. They even tried to use a hair dryer on me. Only God knows what for.

"I am in recovery now, and, believe it or not, I am better. I processed the moments after the rape, and I processed the investigation by the police. I may have done a lot of work, but I'm still afraid to look good, even though I know that had nothing to do with the rape. I am getting past some of the depression, and I don't just lie around. I can go to work most days.

"I do still wake up in the middle of the night, sometimes feeling like the bottom of my stomach is falling out. I've just about stopped the uncontrollable crying, but sometimes I still start to cry for seemingly no reason at all.

"Lots of things are better, but now I have romantic obsessions, like thinking my knight in shining armor will protect me. I had a good daddy and wasn't molested as a child, but I long for some magical quality in someone so I will feel complete. I am unable to joke at all about most things. I lost my last boyfriend because he said I was too possessive and clinging. I tried to do better, but really didn't understand what I was doing with him. I know I was too dependent on him, but I was confused and still kept looking for someone even while I was hoping maybe he was already there. I know now this isn't intimacy, it's pain. I am learning to get past all of this. I hope to really trust one day, but it is so hard now."

Commitment and Intimacy

One husband I worked with, whose wife had been raped by a neighbor many times when she was a child, describes how happy he was the first time he saw his wife as a whole person, not just as a sexual being. It is truly wonderful to see the tenderness between these two people at this time. She wept at the knowledge that somehow he saw her just as a person. She drew ever closer to him, not just physically, but also in being able to give her heart to him.

There are many challenges for the victim of abuse in the area of sexual relations, but God's Word is a place to start seeking for deep revelation. Genesis 4:1 (KJV) says, "And Adam knew Eve his wife and she conceived and bare Cain." The word used here in the Hebrew to depict a sexual relationship is *know*. The primary meaning of this verb is "to see." It means to perceive by sight and by touch, but chiefly in the mind; hence to understand. A second meaning carried by this Hebrew word is "to come to knowledge by seeing, by hearing, and by experiencing." A third meaning is "to know that which is, or has not been known before." Still another meaning is "to know how and to understand." This word has seven other meanings, according to William Wilson's *Old Testament Word Studies*.* It is my prayer that you will pray to know what God has for you to understand about your own sexual intimacy.

Intimacy has the overwhelming challenge of commitment. But as far as I can see, there is no greater expression of love than the deep intimacy of knowing. Knowing another and being known is to destroy the darkness. This is intimacy; this is love.

---

*William Wilson, *Old Testament Word Studies* (Grand Rapids, MI: Kregel Publications, 1980).

WORKBOOK

1. What do you believe to be the greatest barriers to your ability for intimacy?

2. What is there in your life from which you believe you need restoration in order to be able to risk intimacy?

3. In what unproductive ways have you attempted to get your intimacy needs met? Describe the results.

4. As you read the declaration on pages 176–77 every day for one week, what emotions did it arouse in you? Describe those feelings. Were there parts that were difficult for you to believe? Why?

5. Review the list of Probable Causes for Emotional Isolation on page 177. Describe the ways in which you learned to shut down emotionally, including any areas not mentioned in the list.

6. What were your emotional reactions to the realization that your intimacy needs have not been met? Describe them in some detail.

7. Describe what intimacy has meant to you in the past and what it means now. How does the expanded meaning of the Hebrew word *know* help your understanding of intimacy?

8. Describe your sexual behavior as a single person and as a married person (if applicable). What impact has sexual intimacy had upon your life?

9. Describe the effect of your spouse's attitude and behavior on your ability to be emotionally, mentally, and physically intimate. What would you say to your spouse that would better equip him or her to help you in your recovery? To your children? To your family? To a close friend? Describe in detail.

10. What does the scripture found in the heading of this chapter, Luke 11:35–36, mean to you? Explain.

14.

Defying the Darkness—
Confrontation and the Perpetrator

Will Thy wonders be made known in the darkness?
And thy righteousness in the land of forgetfulness?
—Psalm 88:12, NASB

Victims of sexual abuse often feel great helplessness in dealing with any issues concerning the perpetrator. The purpose of this chapter therefore is to present facts about the abuser and to help you determine the confrontation method you will need for your recovery. It is to be understood from the outset that there is no intent to minimize or discount the effects of your abuse nor to vindicate the perpetrator. No one can justify the vicious crime of sexual abuse. Certainly I am not taking the side of the aggressor nor ignoring the devastating results of the sexual abuse in your life.

Victims are often overwhelmed with fear at the thought of their perpetrator(s). The fear and its accompanying helplessness are closely interconnected with the perpetrator. As victims become aware of the truth about their perceived helplessness, they gain strength, and as their recovery gradually progresses they find that fear has disappeared and been replaced by God's wisdom. It is this wisdom that will help you understand the recommended method of confrontation.

What If You're Not Ready for a Confrontation?

Should you feel unable to read this chapter now, it is all right; please put it aside. This book is intended to help you in

192

your recovery, and should not be read or studied until you feel ready for each new challenge. For the present, try to write out what you are feeling, along with any reasons you can identify for not wanting to discuss the idea of confrontation, and talk it out with a professional.

A common reaction to the subject of confrontation is anger. You may even have felt angry just at reading the word *perpetrator*. This, of course, is all right, too. If, as you *can* read through this chapter, you will make notes when you feel especially angry, they will help in your eventual confrontation. If your anger is consuming you, reread chapter 9, which deals with overcoming anger. Then at a later time try again to read this present chapter.

When Others Rally 'round the Perpetrator

A realistic problem for victims is that everybody seems to rally around the perpetrator. Many of my clients have said in sessions with me, "All he has to do is say he is sorry, and everybody wants to treat him great!" Unfortunately, this is all too common. Many family systems invite the perpetrator to the family activities but exclude the victim. Whether intended or not, revictimization of the victim is inevitable in this situation. Often the attitude is that the victim needs to hurry up and forgive and get the family together again—a grave mistake that can often increase recovery time by causing the victim to feel abandoned again. Recovery takes a long time in any case, but the process can be shortened in a Christ-centered in-hospital treatment program. Unfortunately, for many a minimum of two years is needed to process this most horrendous crime of sexual abuse.

What Forgiveness Has to Do with Confrontation

Please remember as you read this chapter that confrontation is a very important part of your recovery. Remember also, that the perpetrator who is in his or her own recovery program may seek your forgiveness. Do not feel that you are forced to extend it. When you are ready, God will show you His grace and aid in forgiving.

The psalmist in Psalm 88:12 asks the difficult question, *Can God's blessings be known in the darkness?* The answer, of course, is yes. God's wonders can be known not only to the victim, but to the perpetrator as well. Some of my counselees react very negatively to hearing me say that God's wonders can be known by the perpetrator, and it is perfectly acceptable for you to feel that way too. These emotions just say that God has not yet completed restoring you; your soul is still deeply afflicted by the abuse. God's love will in time restore you. But, for now, please remember that we have a loving God who does not desire that any should perish.

Verse 12 of Psalm 88 also tells us that God's righteousness (right standing) is in "the land of forgetfulness" (NASB). This image becomes clearer when we remember that one of the translations of the Hebrew verb *to forgive* is "forget." It is a fact that the perpetrator cannot give back to you what he or she took, but *God* will and can. Even though the perpetrator is responsible for the aggression, God gives him/her the freedom to enter the land of forgetfulness and to choose to ask for forgiveness.

Forgiveness that results in healing is not just the deep sorrow that Judas felt about his sin, but the true repentance that the prodigal son experienced in his willingness to risk even humiliation in order to be restored. His decision produced a true change in his life. The Hebrew language describes *repentance* as a "grieving for the evil a person has brought upon another." This is the challenge for the perpetrator. The prodigal son knew, as did Judas, that he had sinned against heaven and against his father, and he felt that he was no longer worthy to be called a son. It was a long road back from a distant land to his father's house, but he took responsibility and traveled the road.

Understanding Perpetrators

Many perpetrators will not travel the road back to their Father's house nor choose the road to recovery. Some who start the road to recovery will not put forth the hard work that is necessary to complete the journey, while others will only pretend to start a recovery program in order to avoid prosecution. Still others will say a recovery process is not necessary because the abuse never happened. An excellent book from which to get further help in understanding perpetrators is *A Betrayal of Innocence* by David B. Peters.*

Elsewhere we have already noted that perpetrators are "me first" individuals who think of their own pleasure. Some have dominant personalities and may exercise tyrannical control of their homes. Often they are unable to have meaningful relationships with persons in their own age group. They are usually emotionally dependent upon others and unable to express their emotional needs appropriately.

Just as with victims, perpetrators can be male or female, adolescents or adults, rich or poor. Perpetrators can be fathers, mothers, brothers, sisters, baby-sitters, uncles, aunts, neighbors, or strangers. Perpetrators can be doctors, pastors, lawyers, teachers, as well as vagrants. They can come from any place within the family and from any place within society. It is interesting to note that the work of David Finkelhor and Diana Russell states that men are responsible for 95 percent of cases of molestation of girls and 80 percent of cases of abuse with boys.**

Personality characteristics frequently found in perpetrators include poor impulse control and low self-esteem. Often offenders are involved with some type of substance abuse and are full of self-pity. They often use pornography, both for

---

*David B. Peters, *The Betrayal of Innocence* (Dallas: Word Publishing, 1986).

**Ronald D. Keelly, "Conspiracy of Silence: Sexual Abuse of Children," in *The Plain Truth*, July 1990, p. 16.

their own stimulation and for attracting possible victims. They may have been emotionally deprived in childhood and may also have been victims themselves. Possibly they have had a great deal of responsibility in their families of origin.

Perpetrators may come from family systems that did not set appropriate boundaries. Often their home situations may be (or may have been) chaotic, with no family members having had their needs appropriately met. Some perpetrators' families may have attempted to isolate their children from the community; some offenders have been extremely overprotected. Their families may sometimes exhibit rigid and extreme religious and moralistic attitudes.

Offenders who have come from an abusive background are not justified in their behavior by that circumstance, but knowledge of the details of that background helps in guiding the offender's recovery process. After all, thousands of victims grow to adulthood and do not perpetrate abuse by actually molesting a child or raping an adult. There is hope for the perpetrator, but the long process of recovery that is required absolutely cannot be taken lightly. The perpetrator's having said "I'm sorry" is simply not enough basis for believing that restoration has occurred. Remember, the abuser made a choice to abuse.

Sexual offense is usually only one aspect of the offender's dysfunctional behavior. If the offense is compounded by evidence of serious psychopathology such as psychosis, substance abuse, or indiscriminate sexual activity manifested in exposing, peeping, or displaying chronic attraction to children, an extensive recovery program is required. Many medical professionals and resource persons in the sexual abuse field find that certain individuals never recover. For example, aggressors who begin pursuing their negative behavior in adolescence and continue into adulthood may simply prefer such a lifestyle and find it too satisfying and pleasurable to give up.

The sexual offender who never takes responsibility but blames the offense on the victim or on the influence of substance abuse is unlikely to benefit from a recovery program. A perpetrator who will not admit the impact the abuse has had on the victim, or a perpetrator who points to the "pleasure" the victim derived from the act, is in complete denial about the crime. These offenders can still receive help in an effective sexual offenders' program, but unless their attitudes are actually changed, they will not recover from their dysfunctional behavior.

An Offender's Story of Recovery

One offender attempts to explain his process of recovery. "I started molesting my stepdaughter when she was about eight years old. At first it was fondling, but later this led into sex. I told her it would hurt, but then it would feel good. It happened just like that. We would drink together. I would buy her everything she wanted. I knew I made her feel special. The school turned me in, and at first I was devastated. I never wanted to hurt her. I loved her. I really did, or at least I thought I did. I began to realize after she started to get help that I really needed her. I started my recovery only because the state forced me to.

"I would tell myself that I knew I needed help but that I wasn't that bad. I would often feel sorry for myself. All I could see were the times my stepdaughter smiled and I made her happy. I was in a group for child molesters, and I hated them. I thought they were all perverts—I wasn't like them. After a year I began to see things a little differently. After many books, after Rapha, after God, I saw what I had really done. I'd always had a lot of self-hate, and that hate got worse before it got better. I have been in recovery now for a couple of years and don't worry about abusing my son or my own daughter. I don't even let myself be alone with them or any children, for that matter.

"I believe I've gotten past the compulsion, but I never, ever, ever want to risk abusing a child again. I never knew what I was doing. Of course, that was only because I didn't want to see it. Well, I see it now, and with God's help, it will never happen again. In my recovery I have learned how to set safe standards with children. I never tickle my daughter any more."

This offender is well on the road to recovery. He committed himself to a long-term recovery program that includes individual, group, and marriage counseling. This man's recovery has progressed because at the point when he felt he had taken a serious look at himself, his behavior, and his feelings, he did not stop but stayed in his recovery process and, like the prodigal son, decided to travel the long distance home.

The Anatomy of Confrontation

Confronting the abuser is a normal part of a recovery program. Confrontations may take place face to face with perpetrators, or in mock confrontations, to be described later in this chapter.

Confrontation should include victims' expressions of how they feel about the effects of their abuse, and how they feel about their perpetrator. In a therapy setting, a perpetrator will often write a letter to the victim taking responsibility for the abuse and seeking forgiveness. Although this is very helpful for the victim, it does not do away with the victim's need to confront the perpetrator with her or his own feelings and emotions.

Confrontation holds extraordinary importance in the family setting, where, for reconciliation to take place, the victim must, in most situations, directly confront the abuser. At disclosure of the perpetration in a family system, all family members, including members of the extended family, need to be informed of the identity of the perpetrator. If it seems harsh that this information should be revealed, consider these two reasons: First, the victim must be protected. Even when a perpetrator starts his or her recovery and is well into that process, it is not uncommon for a relapse to occur. The second reason is to protect all other potential victims in the family system.

What may occur when a victim in a family situation is not protected took place for a teenage daughter who had been abused by her natural father. Both daughter and father had participated in a Rapha in-hospital recovery program. The daughter followed through with an after-care program, but the father did not. Every professional involved in the therapy warned the mother, the daughter, and the father of the potential danger of relapse.

The mother's own words to me affirmed her remorse: "You told me all that could happen and that from that day on I would need to avoid leaving my daughter alone again with her father. You even said I should never leave my future grandchildren alone with their grandfather. I didn't believe you, but now I do."

Fortunately this story has a happy ending, as the daughter stayed in her recovery program and disclosed the relapse of her father to her counselors immediately. The father recommitted to his recovery program. He told me recently, "I am a little scared that maybe my problem is not all over. I like that feeling. In fact, if I weren't a little afraid, I would be worried. The whole family works with me and I with them. When those feelings come I can get immediate support within my family. Sometimes I feel I will never get out of counseling, but I don't care because I know I really need the help."

As to avoiding further victimization of an innocent child by a family perpetrator, I am sorry to report that often I have clients come in for the first time because counseling is needed for their child who has been abused by a grandfather. This grandfather is also the mother's or father's perpetrator.

The same situation holds true in the case of children who have been brought in because of having been molested by their teacher. *Almost always there are other victims.*

Disclosure also allows every family member to be a support to the recovery process of both the victim and the perpetrator. There is absolutely no intent to shame the perpetrator or to provide information about the victim. It is extremely important to honor the victim's privacy concerning the abuse. However, it is also necessary to provide some facts about the perpetrator and the nature of the abuse so that all opportunities for recovery will be available to the victim and to those involved in the counseling.

Confrontation can also be extremely emotional for both the perpetrator and the victim. I strongly recommend that when an actual confrontation with a perpetrator is to take place, it should be with the help of a professional who has worked in the areas of sexual abuse and sexual addiction.

Victims must prepare themselves for possible rejection at the confrontation. Most abusers condemn those who confront them. In many states, children as young as five must face their perpetrators in court. This often revictimizes the young victim, so it is of utmost importance to be very careful and mindful of confrontation.

Mock confrontation is another form of confrontation often used in therapy sessions. This kind of confrontation is in no way a mockery. It has such reality for victims that they are enabled to release the painful emotions of abuse. A safe environment in which to have this confrontation take place is absolutely essential. In physical terms, the victim may confront an empty chair, a picture of the perpetrator, or any other association-producing object or setting that will create a feeling of reality. This method allows the victim to confront the perpetrator as if he or she were actually present. This is a major step in the recovery of victims because it enables them to release the emotions stuffed inside them and begin to regain the power they lost to the abuser. Again, I believe the need for the presence of a professional in this kind of confrontation is just as important as it is for the other types already discussed in this chapter. This is clearly indicated by the emotional intensity a mock confrontation generates.

Reconciliation: Unity and Peace

Joseph was reconciled with his brothers when they came to Egypt in search of grain. The Greek word for *reconcile* means "to change from one condition to another, so as to remove all enmity and leave no impediment to unity and peace." By the time Joseph's brothers reached Egypt, he was able to stand before them—confront them—with no feelings inside him that would keep him from having a relationship of unity and peace with them.

It is God's will that unity and peace be within you also. If direct confrontation is to be a part of your recovery process, seek Him as well as a professional counselor. If reconciliation is to be a part of your process, seek God for restoration of those relationships. But remember, reconciliation will never ever include abuse, only peace and unity.

If the perpetrator has tried to know God's wonders and to enter the land of forgetfulness (referred to in our discussion of Ps. 88:12 early in this chapter), he will have asked God to pardon his sin. He will have sought your forgiveness. He may even have tried to make atonement by supporting your recovery financially; for example, by paying for your counseling. You can be assured that in the land of forgetfulness the perpetrator will experience a deep grieving about what he or she has done to you.

Typical Reactions of Perpetrators to Confrontation

Remorse

It is important in preparing for the confrontation process to understand three typical kinds of reactions from perpetrators. One kind of offender is extremely remorseful. This perpetrator could be a mother, for example, who at some time during her child's infancy kissed or touched the baby's genital area in a sexual manner. This type of offender would have committed the offense only once or twice and may have been wanting for years to ask the victim for forgiveness. He or she is willing to accept the responsibility and is aware of the possible damage the victim has suffered. Another offender could be a young girl or boy who has fondled a younger child, with intercourse not having been a part of the offense and the offense having happened only once or twice. Such offenders have probably carried their guilt and shame for months, even years. The perpetrators in these cases are usually victims themselves, and there is usually genuine repentance. Confronting them generally results in a pleasant ending.

Denial

Most commonly, offenders are in a state of denial and refuse to acknowledge that anything happened. After all, who wants to be labeled a "child molester"? Another obvious reason for the denial is that the abuse is a crime punishable by incarceration. Offenders also feel an intense need to justify and protect themselves from recognizing and feeling the extent of the travesty. Some perpetrators have sociopathic traits, have little guilt, and volubly deny any involvement in such an offense. Their denial is a powerful belief to which they tenaciously cling.

Ralph, an offender of the type just described, still denied committing child abuse even after all the authorities involved on the case explained that absolutely no one believed him; the physical evidence as well as his daughter's statements clearly pointed to him as the perpetrator. His daughter's hymen was not intact, and there was scarring in the vaginal area. She had also made several outcries that were a matter of public record. Ralph's response to overwhelming evidence was, finally, to admit that this "might have happened." He himself did not believe he had done anything to his daughter, and he certainly "didn't remember any such thing." But because the authorities, the therapists, and his daughter said so, he "guessed" he must have done it. Ralph never completed his recovery. This type of perpetrator is a great danger to society, as he will very likely victimize someone again.

Another offender, also in denial and having the same history, can be presented with the same set of facts as Ralph had to face but be relieved when the need for disclosure occurs. This individual wants the abuse to stop, even though it has been going on for some time. In no way, however, does his attitude indicate that he will not need an extensive recovery program. Quite the contrary—the denial in which this perpetrator has been gripped requires treatment just as urgently as someone like Ralph.

Paula, after a year of counseling, is about to confront her uncle. Paula has already written a letter in which she and her husband have asked her uncle and his wife to join them at a local restaurant. Before the meeting she sends her uncle a book on sexual abuse victims. Paula and I have prepared a tape that she intends to play to her uncle at the meeting. (I have learned that confronting a perpetrator by using a tape is very effective. The victim is not forced to shut down if the perpetrator becomes verbally or emotionally abusive during the confrontation, and she is also able to include all that she wishes to say to the perpetrator. Another advantage is that if the confrontation becomes too emotional, the victim can shut off the tape and take time for things to settle down.)

During the first part of the meeting, the perpetrator begins to apologize to Paula for what he has done to her. Explaining that both he and his wife had been victims of sexual abuse, he thanks her for the book and again apologizes.

This confrontation was a very moving event that brought healing to both perpetrator and victim. He took responsibility for the offense and asked for her forgiveness. As far as Paula knows, her uncle is still in a recovery program along with his wife. Paula does not wish to have a close relationship with him, and in fact she doesn't care if she ever sees him again. But she counts her confrontation with her abuser as positive and productive in her recovery process. One satisfaction was in being able to ask him why he had abused her. He seemed to have difficulty finding the words to answer, but finally said, "I was just selfish and took what I wanted."

This confrontation had partial benefits, but not all confrontations will be as productive. In fact, ill-timed confrontation or confrontation with certain types of perpetrators may cause a serious setback for the victim, and in some cases may even be dangerous. If your offender blames the abuse on alcohol, drugs, or you, or if he or she belittles the victimization, it is doubtful that a confrontation will enhance your recovery. However, this is something you and a professional will need to decide.

Alyssa, a mother of two, got a call that her father was in the hospital and about to die. Her counselor thought that confrontation might be a little premature, but Alyssa had an adamant desire to confront her father. She flew out to see him for the last time and to confront him. This was only a few weeks before his actual death, so she also prepared herself for the guilt that she might feel over this confrontation.

At the hospital, after a brief time of polite conversation, she asked him why he had molested her. He looked straight at her and said, "The reason I molested you is that from the time you were a baby I knew you wanted me. Whenever I would change your diaper, you would kick up your legs at me. You would just smile and I knew in my heart that you wanted to have sex with me." Alyssa's anger—and disbelief—soared as high as her body would allow. Venting her rage and disgust toward her father and toward his denial, she told him in considerable detail what she really experienced from his abuse.

Even in his terminal condition, he never accepted the responsibility and never admitted committing any offense. Alyssa nevertheless felt better and was extremely glad that she had confronted him. The event worked for her, but confrontation with a perpetrator who is in total denial doesn't always turn out so well. In Alyssa's case, some positive factors had their effect. Her mother had previously flown into the area where Alyssa lived and participated in her daughter's recovery program. Also, Alyssa was well down the road of recovery when she received the call about her father. She believes the confrontation helped her understand how sick he really was.

Denial of the type Alyssa encountered usually devastates the victim. This is particularly true if the victim is already full of self-blame and is seeking the confrontation solely in order for the abuser to take the responsibility of the abuse. Unfortunately, the abuser seldom makes the response the victim desires.

Mistaken Interpretation and Further Victimization

A third type of offender is one who admits to the offending behavior and unswervingly protests that it is not a crime. This perpetrator believes he or she is actually helping by teaching the child how to have sex, in fact improving the quality of life for the child. This person is a pedophile, an offender who deliberately sets up situations in which children can be victimized. Confrontation is usually not effective, as this person may well be a sociopath who feels no remorse, and it is more than likely that the victim will be revictimized in a confrontation.

These perpetrators not only have no remorse, but often approve of those who participate in victimizing. Romans 1:29–32 (NASB) may describe these individuals quite well. It describes them as being "filled with all unrighteousness, wickedness, greed, evil, full of envy, murder, strife, deceit, malice; they are gossips, slanderers, haters of God, insolent, arrogant, boastful, inventors of evil, disobedient to parents, without understanding, untrustworthy, unloving, unmerciful, and although they know the ordinances of God, that those who practice such things are worthy of death, they do not only do the same, but also give hearty approval to those who practice them."

Confrontation and Perpetrators of Ritualistic Abuse

Victims of ritualistic abuse have almost certainly experienced the horror of being abused by just such perpetrators as described in Romans. These victims cannot physically confront their perpetrators for various reasons. Often the aggressors are unknown to the victim. Perhaps the victim was drugged during the abuse. Perhaps the abuse occurred in a ritual child-dedication ceremony and is lost in the victim's memory. Many possible reasons could be listed, but even if these perpetrators could actually be found and confronted, they would only attempt to abuse again. In such cases, we rely on mock confrontation because the Word of God says specifically not to have anything to do with such evil.

Other Dangerous Perpetrators

The description in Romans does not apply just to satanic ritualistic abuse, but may also fit other perpetrators. Rapists may have many of the characteristics listed in that scripture. If you have been a victim of a perpetrator displaying such characteristics, use these verses to confront your abuser on their effects in your life. (Prefer mock confrontation in most cases; great caution is required in face-to-face encounters with unstable minds.) A teenager describes the abuse she endured from her cousin. "He was evil and wicked. He would watch pornographic movies to get new ideas to abuse me. He would never show mercy when I would cry and beg him to stop. I would give him money so he would not hurt me again. He would take the money and do it anyway. I couldn't trust him. He would invent his own evil. He had no understanding and no love within him, yet every Sunday there he was in church. He was full of deceit in every way."

Tanya, a fifteen-year-old female, describes the terror of being anally raped by her criminally insane perpetrator. He was caught and sent to a mental health facility for the criminally insane. She had to process overwhelming dread and recurrent feelings of panic, as he had broken into her home in broad daylight. She worked many months to get past the damaging fear that had resulted from her powerlessness to stop the rape. Finally she was able to write a letter of confrontation giving him the responsibility of the rape. After a period of time she was able to read the letter to an empty chair during a mock confrontation. After a further period of time she was able to express her anger and describe what she deeply felt about the rape.

The Perpetrator's Apology Session

A confrontation with a perpetrator can also be a first step to the perpetrator's apology session. The victim and perpetrator can meet with a professional and the victim can confront the perpetrator in a safe environment. The perpetrator at some point in the recovery needs to meet with the entire family and ask forgiveness from each member. This is a very difficult session, and often the victim may feel somewhat embarrassed. Also, other siblings may want to avoid the issuesif they feel unable to cope with the situation.

As difficult as this process is, it may keep the spouse and siblings in an incestuous family from being second (and further) victims. An eight-year-old boy told me how jealous he was of his dad for going into his sister's room so often. He wasn't quite sure why, but he felt confused and angry that she was getting all the attention. His thirteen-year-old brother says he just wants to forget about it, as it was too painful to even think about what his dad did with his sister.

These apology sessions require a great deal of effort on the part of each family member. But please remember that one of the primary blocks to recovery is "keeping the secret." Another block is denial. All the members of the family need to process their own individual denials. This same principle applies within the alcoholic family, where each member must come to grips with what has actually happened within their family system. Such honesty will produce life, not death, for the family unit and for each family member.

The Decision to Confront

Let me encourage you to confront your perpetrator. Decide whether what you have learned points toward a personal confrontation or a mock one, but use it to release your feelings of hurt and anger. Make a decision to face the perpetrator with the result of his or her crime. However, you need the help of a professional to decide when to confront and whether the confrontation should be done personally or symbolically. To repeat, it is extremely important for confrontation to take place in a safe environment and to have potential support from other people. If you have more than one abuser, confront each one of them individually. Don't rationalize, apologize, or make excuses for them, but directly confront the aggressor concerning the effects of the abuse in your life. Confront him or her with your honest feelings. Remember that each perpetrator made a choice to abuse. You make a choice to confront.

Mixed Feelings

A final area that many victims need to explore is that of their own mixed feelings toward their perpetrator. The presence of mixed feelings is a common phenomenon in situations where the perpetrator is a family member or is a highly valued person, such as a youth pastor or an inspiring teacher. For example, if the abuser is a father, the victim may have many conflicting emotions from loathing to loving, particularly if the father had been relatively nurturing and supporting for a number of years before the actual abuse began. At any rate, the victim must sort through these contradictory emotions and feelings.

For the victim of rape by a stranger, the presence of mixed feelings is not likely to occur. However, this victim should still be mindful of feelings and emotions and not sweep any of them under the spiritual rug. As Christians, we sometimes think we have taken care of all our feelings because we want the offender to be with Christ, and we may spend time praying for him. Certainly we may reach this point in our thinking, but we do need to respect all the emotions God has given us as individuals and process any damaging emotions we may discover.

It is fairly easy to understand that a child would want the attention and affection of a father and a mother. After all, that is what God intended. Some child victims seem to have a very strong attachment to their perpetrators and want to protect them from any consequences of their abusive behavior. These victims do want the *abuse* to stop, but they do not want the *relationship* to stop. What they really want and have always wanted is a healthy, caring relationship.

These young victims have a burden of inner turmoil about their mixed feelings of love and hate. This is probably all right for the *most* part. However, it is extremely important to evaluate any feelings toward the perpetrator of helplessness, pity, sorrow, and the like. This is an area that must be processed if a healthy attitude toward the perpetrator is to be developed. The feelings that must be discovered and examined may be as unhealthy as hate that never leads to forgiveness or fear that submerges honest responses to putdowns and false assumptions. Victims, to become overcomers, must not only assign accountability to the perpetretator verbally and physically, but emotionally as well. They are no longer the caretakers of the perpetrator.

At the start of their journey to recovery, many victims have anger and hatred toward the perpetrator. But as these individuals begin to overcome these negative feelings, they start to recognize some positive feelings. These victims may begin to remember very pleasant times with the perpetrator. Often this is frightening to them. But please remember, if you were a little girl or a little boy with a father or grandfather as perpetrator, you may have been treated very well apart from the abuse, and these feelings are normal. In fact, these are the feelings God wanted you to have in a *healthy* relationship with your caretakers.

Don't Condemn Your Feelings

The point is, please do not feel shame or guilt about these feelings. It is normal for a little child to love a parent. Also remember, perpetrators are almost always known to the seduced victim. This seduction may very well have been a positive experience, even though it was full of deception. You were too young to know that you were being seduced, and consequently you may have enjoyed much of your relationship with the perpetrator. It is perfectly all right to have enjoyed the healthy part of the relationship. And just as you may physically have enjoyed the stimulation, a normal physiological reaction, you would also have enjoyed the healthy emotional stimulation. Sexual abuse not only touches the body, but it also touches the mind.

It is very important in your recovery to deal with all your feelings and experiences involving you and your perpetrator. You will reach a point in your recovery at which you begin grieving the loss of a healthy childhood relationship. For example, you may begin to feel a longing for a daddy, and you may wish for his love. You may have a need to feel special. These feelings were always there. God intended every child to have a nurturing and loving family. Again, please don't condemn yourself for these feelings. Allow God to restore any love, any nurturing, any affection, any hugs that you didn't receive in your childhood.

Words of Comfort

Do not take these feelings of longing for a loving family and suppress them. Instead take them to the cross and grieve for the loss of your childhood. In his Second Letter to the Corinthians, Paul speaks of the comfort God sent him in the coming of Titus: "But God, who comforts the depressed comforted us . . ." (2 Cor. 7:6, NASB). He will comfort you also, and He will restore the lost love of your broken heart.

WORKBOOK

1. What is your attitude about your perpetrator? List the similarities of your perpetrator to the characteristics found in Romans 1:29–32 (see p. 205).

2. How do you feel about your perpetrator(s)? Angry? Sad? Accepting? Forgiving? Afraid? Loving? Protective? Answer with these and other one-word or brief descriptions.

3. Write a letter to your perpetrator(s) telling all the effects of your abuse. Express how you really feel about him/her/them. Also express how you really feel about the abuse. Finally, describe how you feel all over.

4. How would you feel if your perpetrator(s) blamed you for the abuse at a confrontation? What might you do? What might you wish to do?

5. Project an image of an actual or mock confrontation with your perpetrator(s). What would you want from your perpetrator(s) through the confrontation? What do you believe you would receive from the perpetrator(s) in an actual confrontation?

6. How do you think you would react if your perpetrator(s) denied that the abuse ever happened? Has the abuse already been denied by your perpetrator(s)? If so, what did he/she/they say? How did you feel?

7. Are any of your family members aware of the abuse? If they are, how have they responded to you? If not, how does that affect your relationship?

8. How would you prepare yourself for a possible confrontation (or confrontations)?

9. This question does not assume that reconciliation should or will occur, but asks that you describe what feelings you have within you if the possibility were to arise. Try to probe deeply for possible buried feelings.

10. Read Psalm 88. In terms of confronting your perpetrator(s), what special meaning does verse 12 have for you?

15.
Staying in the Light—
A Message for Friends and Helpers

"You . . . are a guide to the blind, a light to those who are in darkness."

Romans 2:19, NASB

Through this final chapter, I hope to help not only the victims of abuse, but also their friends (including relatives of all degrees of closeness) and helpers (including therapists and other caregivers). By the time they have reached maturity, most victims have been revictimized many times. Also by the time of maturity, most will have abused others, at the least by being overly angry. Accordingly, the most precious gift of this chapter would be to impart truth to all readers—truth that would produce life for each individual.

What Not to Say

First let's look at the list on page 216 entitled "The Don'ts." There are fifteen statements in this list, all of them words that family members, close friends, or even professional caregivers might say to a sexual abuse victim, but shouldn't. Sometimes these statements are made because the friend who made them has absolutely no understanding of sexual abuse issues. Other times the person making them may be mentally exhausted with the victim or the recovery process. Still other individuals simply may not wish to deal with this difficult situation, because it is threatening to them and consumes too much time.

Whatever the reasons are for making any of these "don't" statements, they must be recognized for what they are—statements that bring darkness, a kind of death, to the victim. There is a time when the victim must leave the past, but premature admonitions to forgive and forget can be very destructive.

All too often these statements are made at the moment of discovery of the abuse or during the difficult days of the healing process. The most important gift you can give the

---

"The Don'ts"

Don't say to the victim:

1. I don't believe you were ever abused.
2. Why can't you just forget it?
3. That's in the past. Why keep bringing it up?
4. Can't you just let go? It's not happening now.
5. Why are you making such a big deal? You were only three.
6. Just pray about it. Give it to God.
7. You are the problem, not what happened.
8. Why didn't you stop it?
9. Stop thinking about it. It's a sin. The Bible says to think on things that are good.
10. What did you do to cause it to happen?
11. Why can't you hurry up and get over this?
12. Paul said to forget the past and to move on toward the future.
13. You're not forgiving. You have to forgive or God won't help you.
14. I am so sick of this. What about me?
15. You have got to quit feeling sorry for yourself.

victim is the time to heal. If you are a close friend or relative you may need to find support yourself, but nevertheless, please give the victim the time he or she needs for recovery.

The list on the previous page contains only a few possible "don'ts." Of course the list could have been longer, but the important thing is that both victims and friends or helper be willing to work on the "don'ts." Most individuals involved with sexual abuse victims have no understanding of the possible severity of these statements for the victim. Such statements can also be very painful for the friends and families of victims due to the deep emotional scars inflicted by sexual abuse. This is not a reason to place blame or to allow someone not to take responsibility. Conversely it is for the victim and the friend of the victim to be accountable in the relationship to the best of their ability.

Dealing with Injuries That Can't Be Seen

If the person injured by the abuse had been left with broken arms and legs as the result of a car accident, friends would rush to help. And most people, even casual acquaintances, would in the short run be willing supporters during the victim's healing process. But if recovery were to take a long, long time, even a willing participant might grow weary.

Another real problem for friends of a victim is that they can't see the brokenness of the heart whereas the brokenness of the bone is evident, by x-ray if not by outward appearance. The heart of a victim is truly shattered, but unfortunately, there is no x-ray to show to friends.

The Demands of Giving

At the early stage of the sexual abuse victim's recovery, friends may be called to give more than the victim. Often the victim is simply not capable. One husband and wife came to my office because the wife did not want to have sexual intercourse with her husband. She was in denial as a result of the abuse, and he was very angry. He didn't want to pay for the counseling and didn't want to participate in the therapy. In this particular recovery program, abstinence from sex is necessary for a period of time. He was only agreeable to letting his wife be in the program because, as he said, "Well, that's what's happening anyway—so it couldn't be any worse." Fortunately, in spite of his initial reluctance, the husband was able to reach deep inside himself in order to help his wife. God was able to touch their lives, although during the early part of the wife's recovery, she simply was not functioning. This story ended in a great victory for both husband and wife.

She said, "I can't believe sex is really good. But, Cindy, I never knew or understood the intimacy that God intended for me through sex. How distorted it was for me in the past, but now the most beautiful part is how tenderly my husband sees me. I want to say it is a miracle, but I realize this is really just how God meant it to be."

This husband chose to support, accept, and understand. He and his wife certainly had ups and downs in the process of recovery, but they chose to forgive and try again and again to continue on their long road out of darkness. The important thing was that this husband chose to show interest in his wife's recovery. He didn't just look at her as the problem, but he saw *they* had a problem—a problem he came to understand as sexual abuse. He also learned that he needed to grow as a Christian and become part of the healing process. God blessed this couple mightily because, in the midst of the hurt and anger, they chose not to give up. They chose to recover.

How to Help

Not every victim's story ends so beautifully, of course. But friends of a victim can help make that happen by following the "Dos," listed in the box on the following page. Many others are sure to suggest themselves to you also.

"The Dos"

Do stand ready . . .

1. To give support.
2. To give acceptance.
3. To give love.
4. To give time.
5. To give understanding.
6. To give interest.
7. To give forgiveness.
8. To give help.
9. To give belief.
10. To give prayer.
11. To give encouragement.
12. To give hope.
13. To give honor.
14. To give trust.
15. To give validation.

Handling Emotions That Friends Feel

There are many emotions the friend of a victim may experience as well. For example, if you are a mother or a father and discover that your child was raped, you may have a great deal of anger. At first it may be directed toward the rapist, then toward yourself, and sometimes even toward the victim. This is often a normal pattern of response. I have seen more than one "big, tall Texas man" cry at the victimization of his wife or daughter. I have seen the tears turn to hatred. Learning of the abuse of a loved one is difficult for the family and the friends of a victim. If this has happened to you, find someone who will help you through your pain, guilt, and anger. This help can also allow you to be more effective in the support you want to give to your individual loved one.

I am ending this chapter with the hope that in some way friends and victims will help each other during the healing process. I cannot begin to describe how much difference there is between the progress of a victim who receives support and one who does not. But I can make this statement with great certainty: Loving support will almost always reduce the recovery time for the victim. This support is not measurable, just as God's love is not measurable.

A Final Prayer

In the workbook section I have asked the victim to read you, the friend, a letter. Take a second step of support by truly listening. You have already taken the first by reading this book. I pray that God will let you know His will and approve those things that are essential to the recovery. I pray also that you will, as a friend, be able to "hang onto" godly wisdom in the support process. And I pray that God will build your confidence so that He may use you as light to your special one who is coming out of the darkness.

May God richly bless you
in this
recovery process.

WORKBOOK

1. What "don'ts" from the list on page 216 or other well-meant but hurtful things have people said to you? How did you feel about these remarks at the time they were said? Do any of these still bother you? If so, how?

2. Write letters to people who have made these statements, describing your hurt and pain to them.

3. Read these letters to any significant person who is part of your recovery process. Share your experiences with someone.

4. Write a letter to family and friends requesting the support you need. Be specific.

5. Write a letter to yourself forgiving yourself for having abused anyone as a result of any of the following reactions to your abuse, for example: 1) anger; 2) rigidity; 3) jealousy; 4) lack of intimacy; 5) distrustfulness.

6. Write a letter of apology or reconciliation to everyone you feel you have abused as a result of your reactions to your own abuse.

7. Read the words from Romans 2:19 that are found on page 215 in the heading of this final chapter, "Staying in the Light." Describe what those words mean to you.

8. Describe your feelings about whatever support you received as a child, and also as an adult. Also include your feelings about lack of support in those same two periods of your life. Was the support appropriate? If not, why was it inappropriate? Describe the harmful effects it may have had. Who supported you?

9. Describe your feelings toward God's support of you during your victimization. Describe your feelings toward God's support of you during recovery.

10. Read the Book of John, circling the word *love* in your Bible every time you see it. Pray John 17 every day for one week. Promise never, ever, to forget that right now Jesus is praying for you.

List of
Suggested Readings
and Resources

BOOKS

Allen, Dr. Charles. *God's Psychiatry*. Old Tappan, NJ: Fleming H. Revell Co., 1953.

Allender, Dan B. *The Wounded Heart*. Colorado Springs, CO: NavPress, 1990.

Backus, William, and Marie Chapian. *Telling Yourself the Truth*. Minneapolis, MN: Bethany House, 1980.

Buhler, Rich. *Pain and Pretending*. Nashville, TN: Thomas Nelson, 1988.

Courtois, Christine. *Healing the Incest Wound*. New York: W. W. Norton, 1988.

Elliott, Lynda D., and Vicki L. Tanner, Ph.D. *My Father's Child: Help and Healing for the Victims of Emotional, Sexual, and Physical Abuse*. Brentwood, TN: Wolgemuth & Hyatt, Publishers, 1988.

Frank, Jan. *A Door of Hope*. San Bernardino, CA: Here's Life Publishers, Inc., 1987.

Hancock, Maxine, and Karen Burton Mains. *Child Sexual Abuse: A Hope for Healing*. Wheaton, IL: Harold Shaw, Publisher, 1987.

McGee, Robert S., and Dr. Harry Schaumburg. *Renew: Hope for Victims of Sexual Abuse*. Houston: Rapha Publishing, 1990.

McGee, Robert S. *The Search for Significance*. Houston: Rapha Publishing, 1990.

Morrison, Jan. *A Safe Place: Beyond Sexual Abuse*. Wheaton, IL: Harold Shaw, Publisher, 1990.

Peters, David B. *A Betrayal of Innocence*. Dallas, TX: Word, 1986.

Sandford, Paula. *Healing Victims of Sexual Abuse*. Tulsa, OK: Victory House, 1988.

Springle, Pat. *Codependency*, 2d ed. Houston and Dallas, TX: Rapha/Word, Inc., 1990.

Stratford, Lauren. *Satan Underground*. Eugene, OR: Harvest House, 1988.

Vine, W. E. *An Expository Dictionary of New Testament Words.* Old Tappan, NJ: Fleming H. Revell Co., 1966.

Webster's New Collegiate Dictionary. Springfield, MA: G. & C. Merriam Co., 1974.

Wilson, William. *Old Testament Word Studies.* Grand Rapids, MI: Kregel Publications, 1980.

ORGANIZATIONAL RESOURCES

Rapha, Inc., 8876 Gulf Freeway, Houston, TX 77017 (800-383-HOPE) provides Christ-centered inpatient psychiatric and substance abuse programs in various cities throughout the country. Offers a toll-free number for emergencies, assessment, and a Sexual Issues Helpline.

GROUP STUDY RESOURCES

To obtain copies of *The Search for Significance, Codependency,* or *Your Parents and You* books, workbooks, and leader's guides, contact Rapha, Inc. at 8876 Gulf Freeway, Suite 340, Houston, TX 77017.

For further information on support groups, Rapha Conferences, and seminars, call Rapha at 1-800-383-HOPE.

Appendix
Part 1: Leading a Support Group

As we already know, many women and men in the church have been victims of sexual abuse and incest. These victims need the support of compassionate and caring Christians to help in the recovery process and how it impacts their view of themselves. They need help to experience healing.*

Part 1 of this appendix gives direction on leading a support group. Part 2 is a set of twelve lessons to use in a sexual abuse group. In addition, information is listed about other materials published by Rapha which will help victims gain a sense of personal worth and significance as well as insight into their relationships with other adults, their children, and their parents, and with God.

At times victims feel hope is lost, especially as they struggle with the burden of abuse, its wounds, and its memories. Their lives have for so long been a struggle to survive, to hide their hurting, and to heal the wounds alone and in their own strength. Many believe God is not to be trusted since He did not protect them from abuse in the first place. Yet, there is hope offered by our Lord. As victims work through these concepts in the context of relationships with God's people who look to His Word and the healing of His Spirit, we pray that their weeping will turn to joy.

---

* This appendix provides a model for helping adults who at some time in their lives have been sexually abused. We acknowledge that both women and men have been sexually abused. Yet, since women more frequently involve themselves in support groups, we will speak to them, at the same time asking that readers keep in mind that most of what we say will also apply to men.

The Importance of Support Groups

Support groups are considered by many mental health professionals to be one of the most important resources in the recovery of a victim of sexual abuse. A group helps the victim develop "a new and living way" from isolation to intimacy to freedom.

The scholars who prepared the special Bible study aids for the Open Bible edition of the *New American Standard Bible* state that the whole purpose of the Book of Hebrews was to inform and encourage the discouraged Christians. People who have been sexually abused also need to be informed and encouraged—informed about the facts of sexual abuse and encouraged in their recovery process. Every victim needs to know that she no longer has to be "only a survivor," but that she now can be an overcomer—even a thriver.

Hebrews 10:25 exhorts us not to "forsake our own assembling together, as is the habit of some, but encouraging one another." There is probably no greater scripture to establish the biblical base and need for a support group. Most victims have established the habit of isolation and have not developed the skills with which to encourage one another.

Qualifications of a Support Group Leader

As has already been explained, the healing process is built upon several principles: (1) the sexual abuse victim must acknowledge her victimization and the reality of the resulting hurt and pain; (2) she must understand her patterns of relating to other people that result from her victimization; and (3) she must learn new patterns of giving and receiving love. As love casts out the fear that has been so pervasive in her life and healing begins, she can be freed to move toward others with warmth and kindness. She will also experience the freedom to respond to another's love on a deeper level.

The qualifications for leading others in this process are stringent. Professional education alone is not adequate. Nor does the fact of having suffered sexual abuse by itself qualify a person as a group facilitator. Training, knowledge, and skills are essential for all, but these qualifications must be balanced with experience. Most of all, a sexual abuse support group facilitator needs the maturity to encourage others and to endure difficulties with patience.

The minimum qualifications for a sexual abuse support group facilitator should include all the attributes listed in one or the other of the two following paragraphs:

1. A professionally trained counselor (1) should have had one or more years of counseling experience as a master's level counselor, in which clients have included adults who were victims of sexual abuse; (2) should have completed formal and informal study of the topic of sexual abuse and reading of the resources recommended on page 230; and (3) should be willing to seek more training if needed.

2. A lay person in counseling who has been a victim of sexual abuse (1) should have spent two years in a formal or informal recovery process that has included professional counseling and participation in a support group for victims of sexual abuse; (2) should have been out of recovery for at least two years; (3) should recognize his or her limitations; and (4) should be aware of resources within the community and have read the resources mentioned on page 230.

Adhering to these recommendations will help you and your group avoid serious problems. Helping victims of sexual abuse is not an easy task even for the professional. We hope to avoid the possibility that inadequately prepared facilitators may inadvertently lead participants to experience unnecessary degrees of pain, minimize key issues, underestimate levels of need, or respond inappropriately in a crisis.

The use of this book in a support group is not a substitute

for training in the area of sexual abuse therapy, nor should participating in a support group be considered therapy or a replacement for therapy. A support group is an adjunct to therapy, not therapy itself. Discussions of sexual abuse are frank, explicit, and potentially disconcerting for everyone involved.

If you should question your adequacy to lead a sexual abuse support group, I strongly recommend that you first lead a group using the materials developed for use with the books *Search for Significance, Codependency,* or *Your Parents and You.* These resources are available from Rapha,* and each comes with a small-group leader's guide. Though they do not deal directly with sexual abuse, these books address foundational issues for recovery from sexual abuse.

Leading a support group is not something to be taken lightly but requires a very strong commitment.

Handling Crisis

Participants in sexual abuse support groups commonly struggle with anxiety or panic attacks. As they face their pain, perhaps for the first time, they may be overwhelmed by their emotions and memories. For many, the emotions will produce a sensation of being trapped. Most victims of sexual abuse have at some point had suicidal feelings and may again experience such feelings as they go through the healing process. The intensity of dealing with past abuse may cause some to contemplate suicide for the first time.

As participants enter a crisis, it is critical that they be involved with other members of the support group. We highly recommend that the names and phone numbers of all members of the support group, the phone number of your pastor, and Rapha's 24-hour Sexual Issues Helpline (1-800-383-HOPE) be given to each participant.

A form like the one below has been found to be of invalu-

---

*See p. 226 for ordering information.

able help at times of crisis. Each member can be asked to fill one out and keep it beside the telephone. She may also wish to carry a copy in her handbag, since crisis is almost always a part of the healing process in facing the pain of sexual abuse.

MY PLAN FOR MANAGING CRISIS

I must learn to ask for help and be willing to accept help when it is offered. This may sound easy, but it may actually be extremely difficult even to think of what to do or who to call. When I feel overwhelmed with my emotions—anxiety, depression, or suicidal thoughts—I will contact the following individual(s):

I will call_____ at _____.

If that person is not available, I will call_____
at _____ as a backup.

I may also call my pastor at _____or my counselor at

_____.

I may also call the RAPHA 24-Hour Sexual Issues Helpline (1-800-383-HOPE).

Life is worth living because . . .

(If you can't think of any reasons, ask someone who cares about you to help.)

Leading a Support Group

You are preparing for one of the most stimulating and challenging experiences in life: leading a support group. Throughout church history, God has used small groups to strengthen and motivate people. The support and encouragement often found within the group provide an environment where people can be more vulnerable about their weaknesses and more open to both believing and applying the truth of God's Word. Leading a group like this profoundly serves the members, and because of your active demonstration of faith and love, gives honor to the Lord.

The purpose of a support group is to provide an environment of love and acceptance in which people can better understand sexual abuse and apply the principles of scripture to their lives. *Beyond the Darkness* is designed to help you accomplish this purpose through the use of this appendix and related materials such as those for *The Search for Significance, Codependency,* and *Your Parents and You.*

Material in the workbook sections of each chapter of *Beyond the Darkness* was developed for group study. Open and honest discussions can provide a fertile environment for applying the principles of God's Word to the problem of sexual abuse. As Proverbs 27:17 says, "As iron sharpens iron, so one man sharpens another."

The effectiveness of your efforts will depend on the environment you provide for learning and the amount of desire each group member has for truth. Before looking at the content of each lesson, let's examine some of the principles and particulars of leading a small group:

1. What to expect from your group
2. Ways people learn
3. Asking good questions
4. Preparing to lead your group
5. Tips that make for successful teaching

A careful examination of these points will prepare you to lead your group effectively, so that participants' lives will be changed for the glory of God.

Expectations

What do you expect group members to learn and do as a result of participating in this study? Will they become great theologians, live perfect lives, and/or fulfill the Great Commission in Peru? Thoughts like these may seem ridiculous, yet many of us have misplaced expectations for our groups which can lead to frustration, and even anger.

Basically, our expectations should coincide with the commitment level of our group members. If they sincerely desire to study diligently and be accountable to one another in applying what they learn, then you can expect exciting things to happen! If, on the other hand, their commitment is only to attend group meetings, you will need to lower your expectations.

Regardless of your group's current commitment level, it is important to realize that this may change. God will use your prayers and enthusiasm to impart to others a greater desire to learn and apply these truths in their lives.

The group program developed for *Beyond the Darkness* assumes that each group member will have a copy of the text and at a later time will also study *The Search for Significance, Codependency,* and *Your Parents and You.* Although having all these books is not absolutely necessary, most participants will greatly increase the study's impact if they engage in personal study and reflection on the issues presented in them.

Three general levels of commitment are usually demonstrated by members of small groups:

1. To attend meetings and observe the proceedings without having done any personal study.
2. To read through the questions assigned for the lesson.

3. To work through the assigned questions, writing out answers and applying to their lives the concepts in each lesson.

The third level is by far the most effective. Even if the members of your group begin at the first or second level of commitment, it is to be hoped that they will reach this deepest level of commitment as the weeks progress.

The chart below compares thoughts, feelings, and actions typical of groups at these three different levels. It also suggests activities that may be used by the leader to move the group from one level to the next.

All small groups are not created equal. A group of people who are initially strangers to one another will need to be led differently from a group of friends who know each other very

LEVELS OF COMMITMENT

	GROUP MEMBERS' THOUGHTS AND FEELINGS	GROUP MEMBERS' ACTIONS
Level 1	*Do I belong here? Do they like me? Do I like them?* Anticipation, enthusiasm, anxiety, caution.	Members give only basic information about themselves. Accept others on a superficial basis.
Level 2	*Can I trust these people with my thoughts? What is the direction of the group?* Less enthusiasm, more impatience, anxiety.	Some stop attending. Some become vulnerable and begin to assume the goals of the group.
Level 3	*Let's accomplish something together! I like these people.* Acceptance, freedom, vision, determination.	Members show more commitment to goals, mutual encouragement, and willingness to work through conflict. More leadership is developed.

well. If you understand your group's level, you will be far more likely to meet the real needs of the individual members, to encourage them, and generally to "scratch where they itch."

Ways People Learn

Teachers often assume lesson content is the key to learning. Content, however, is only one of several important factors that determine how well people learn and apply material. In fact, in a recent study, content was found to contribute only 7 percent to what was actually learned! The other 93 percent was comprised of the environment, mood, and mode of expression used in the communication process. Clearly, then,

IN SMALL GROUPS

LEADER'S ATTITUDE AND ACTIONS	LEADER'S PLANNED ACTIVITIES
Warmth, enthusiasm, clear communication about the group's direction.	Uses "ice-breakers" to stimulate interaction. Plans informal time with group leaders. Initiates vulnerability. Uses guided discussion rather than lecture.
Empathy, encouragement, flexibility, honesty. Gets to know members more intimately. Continues to give clear direction.	More open sharing among members, including group prayer, time together outside the group, and involvement in outreach and service.
Encouragement, challenge, clear goals, continued enthusiasm.	Motivates members to initiate outreach and service, and to begin to lead others. Provides training in ministry skills; quality time together outside the group.

the context of the lesson is at least as important as its content.

The following are some requisites for stimulating understanding and application in your small group:

• **Provide the assurance of confidentiality.** As sexual abuse victims begin to recover and are able to participate in group activities, privacy becomes a key factor. All of us need to feel secure, but this is especially true of those who have been victims of sexual abuse.

Holding knowledge about people in confidence builds an atmosphere of trust and security. Emphasize to the group the need for privacy, and make it a requirement that no member should discuss the names or situations of any other group member outside the group itself. A group phone list should be distributed only with the stipulation that phone numbers are *never to be given to a non-group member.* Mention of someone's group attendance to anyone other than a group member or a therapist should be prohibited; and pressure on a group member to attend support group functions should be avoided in the presence of non-group members.

The leader should make it clear that members do not have to give out telephone numbers, even for a class list, and also that no one should hug or touch another member without first asking permission. Each member needs to understand that she has these freedoms.

Every member needs to have complete confidence that none will violate the agreement made in group not to discuss the members or the meetings outside the group itself.

• **Provide an environment of love and acceptance.** Remember that love and acceptance are of tremendous importance to people's ability to learn and communicate. Only when people realize that they aren't going to be criticized or ostracized for giving a wrong answer or for making a "stupid" comment will they feel free to be open and to share their experiences and feelings. Superficial friendliness from the leader is not enough. True love and acceptance are revealed when you exercise patience and understanding even though it would be easier to criticize someone for not doing the assignment, for giving a wrong answer, or for being late to a meeting. Those in your group will be far more likely to understand your lessons on the love of Christ if you demonstrate His unconditional love and acceptance to them.

• **Include the option of participation in extracurricular activities.** Many may think that the group meeting itself is all that is needed to help people learn. However, activities outside the meetings will deepen relationships and provide opportunities for discussing and applying the truths and insights group members are learning. Arranging parties, dinners, games, and retreats, and making phone calls show group members that you really care about them.

If your group is large, you may want to call or meet with different members periodically, or you may want to enlist others in your group to be responsible for some of the calling. Whatever you opt to do, the principle is that learning is greatly enhanced when group meetings are supplemented by outside activities. Recently it was observed that one of the most effective tools of growth is to involve people in outreach and service activities together. Serving and ministering together develop a bond and a vision among members that far surpass what can be gained from sitting in a meeting.

• **Encourage self-discovery.** As helpful as it may be for you to communicate truth to those in your group, they will be even more encouraged if they are allowed to discover it for themselves. Lecturing may be the form of teaching most often used in group studies, but it is one of the least effective. A rich, dynamic learning experience is almost always enhanced when a group comes together to share what they have learned from their own study. Don't feel that you have to be the sole communicator of truth. If group members are doing their own personal study, they will teach one another simply by sharing what they have learned.

• **Include regular prayer time.** A group Bible study can be quite academic until its members pray; then, theories turn into praises and requests, and members can express their genuine needs. Be sure to make prayer a priority, both in the group meetings and in your own preparation for each lesson.

• **Encourage group members to equip themselves to teach a group of their own in the future.** It has been said that the best way to learn is to teach, and that the one who learns the most is the teacher. The people in your group will no doubt receive many fresh insights when they begin to teach a group of their own. They may never have taught before, and they will need your support and guidance, but this will be a rewarding experience for them, *after they have had sufficient preparation*. It is extremely important that they review and follow the guidelines outlined in numbered paragraph 2 on page 229, especially items 1 and 2.

Asking Good Questions

Though each lesson in part 2 of this appendix has specific questions from the workbook sections of *Beyond the Darkness* for you to ask your group, you will benefit by being able to identify three types of questions and understanding the kind of responses they typically generate:

• **Leading questions:** These have an obvious, definite answer, and do not promote discussion. They can, however, be useful if your goal is to obtain a quick, factual answer.

Examples: "Of course you all agree, don't you?" "What does Jesus say in John 10:10?"

• **Limiting questions:** These questions ask people to give a specific answer that is not so obvious, sometimes leading to a mind-reading or guessing game.

Example: "What are the three significant truths of this passage?" *Three? Significant to whom?*

• **Open questions:** Open questions stimulate discovery and interaction. They can ask *who, what, when, where,* or *how.*

Examples: "What do you think of this concept?" "How would you feel in that situation?"

Both leading and open questions are appropriate in some

situations and inappropriate in others. You won't want to ask a leading question when you hope to promote discussion, and you won't want to ask an open question when you need a short, factual answer. A good question is like gold! Learn to be a teacher who knows how to ask good questions.

Preparation

In addition to prayer, the most important preparation for each meeting is to work through and apply the material for yourself. If the Lord is using the material in your own life, you will communicate it with clarity and enthusiasm. Try to work through the questions assigned for the next week as early as possible after giving that assignment to your group. This will allow you time to understand the lesson's concepts better, and to apply its truths to your experience.

When preparing to teach, review the assigned lesson, making your own notes on each aspect of the content. As you work through this material, ask yourself:

- What is the purpose of this lesson?
- Which questions lead to a definite answer?
- Which questions stimulate discussion?
- Are there additional scriptures or questions I want to include?
- What can I do to make the environment more conducive to learning?
- How can I reinforce learning through outside activities?
- What conclusions do I want each person to reach?
- How will the group members apply what they learn?
- *Have I prayed that God will profoundly use this lesson to teach us?*

Adjust the number of questions given for each lesson to the pace and depth of discussion you want to maintain in your meeting. You may need to eliminate some questions. You may want to move rapidly through some of them and spend more time on others. Or, you may have enough time to ask some additional questions.

Tips That Make for Effective Teaching

So many people have learned from their successes and failures in leading small groups that I would be remiss not to include some tips from them here. Applying these insights should help make your teaching more effective:

• **Be sure the scriptures are the basis of discussion.** People's opinions are welcome, but God's Word is the ultimate test of our experience and opinions.

• **Welcome healthy disagreement.** If you aren't threatened by the different perspectives of others, your group will be more open and vulnerable—with you and with each other. Disagreement in an atmosphere of acceptance is very stimulating, but don't let it get out of hand.

• **Try to meet at a time and place that is consistent, comfortable, and relatively free from distractions.** If there is enough time, sharing refreshments can help people mingle and get to know each other. Be careful, however, to keep this activity fairly brief; there have been groups in which it consumed nearly the whole meeting time. You may find it better to make refreshments available at the end of your meeting. Those who are able to stay can then get better acquainted, and those who need to leave can do so.

Select a location for your group meetings where the privacy of members can be protected. This allows victims to express feelings of shame or guilt in a safe environment. Provide comfortable chairs and arrange them in a circle.

• **Be open and vulnerable with your group, so that they will see how the Lord is using the truths of His Word to meet your needs.** At the same time, use discretion in what you say. Try to determine what information will most help your group to understand how the Lord is ministering to you.

• **Stimulate interaction.** Ask "why" questions, or ask, "What do you think?" "What do you feel?" "What do you want?"

• **If someone is quiet, draw her out by asking questions that aren't too difficult.** These might be questions that ask for an opinion, for example, "What do you think about this point?" Then, appropriately affirm her and the answer she has given. Avoid exaggerating your affirmation or it will seem insincere.

• **If the majority of your group doesn't do the assignment, give members a few minutes to reflect on each question before asking for answers.** This will allow group members to consider the issues more fully than they would be able to do if asked to give only a spontaneous response. At the same time, you may want to encourage them to do their own study by explaining how personal study has helped you.

• **If someone comes once or twice to your group but doesn't return, call her to say that you missed her.** Personal concern, not chiding for lack of attendance, is most likely to bring her back.

• **Don't feel that you have to get everyone's response to every question.** Strike a balance between hearing from everyone and moving the meeting along at a healthy pace.

A Profile of Your Small Group

By now, you probably have a good idea of the purpose of this study and the nature of your group. However, it may be helpful to analyze your group specifically to determine your teaching plan. Consider these questions and write down your analysis in the space provided here:

1. How well do the people in your group know each other? What stage is your group in?

2. If those in your group don't know each other well, what "ice-breakers" would be helpful in the first meeting?

3. Will most of the people in your group work through and apply the lesson material weekly? Will they read the questions and discussions, or will they only come and observe?

4. What is the primary need in your group regarding sexual abuse (e.g., fear of rejection, fear of failure, guilt, shame, depression, marriage relationships, etc.)? How can you determine the needs of your group?

5. What activities and interaction outside the group can you plan now that will deepen relationships and stimulate application? (Consider phone calls, parties, and group outreach and service opportunities.)

Other Helps for Evaluating Your Group

Leaders may find that they will be helped in preparing a profile of their group by having the members fill out the questionnaire on pages 244-48 at their first meeting.

Following completion of the group's planned study (or at any time members want to evaluate their progress toward recovery), the Indications of Recovery listed on pages 249–50 provide a good yardstick for measurement.

Ready to Begin

Now you are ready to work with your group! Study diligently, and pray that God will use this study to enable people to understand and relax! He has promised to use His Word powerfully in the lives of His people (Isa. 55:10–11; 2 Tim. 3:16–17; Heb. 4:12–13).

SEXUAL ABUSE SUPPORT GROUP QUESTIONNAIRE

Please complete the following questions and return them to your group facilitator at the beginning of the next meeting. This information will allow your facilitator to become acquainted with you and learn how to respond to your needs. The answers are strictly confidential. Please feel free not to answer any question to which you do not wish to respond.

Name_____

Address_____

Home phone_____Work phone_____

1. Are you aware of sexual abuse in your parents' families? If so, briefly describe.

2. Describe your parents' marital relationship and history.

3. Describe the roles of the other members of your family as well as any role you think you held (e.g., "My sister acted like a mother," "Mom was uninvolved," etc.).

4. What do you recall about yourself as a child growing up? Did you have friends? How well did you get along with others?

5. Describe your sexual abuse as you remember it now. Give such information as when it began; what type of sexual activity was involved and how long the abuse continued; how frequently the abuse occurred; who the perpetrator was and what your relationship with the perpetrator was. Were you given promises or favors, or were you ever threatened?

6. What problems and symptoms are a result of your sexual abuse?

7. Did anyone else know about the sexual abuse? What feelings do you have about their knowing about it?

8. When was your first outcry? (If you have never told anyone about the abuse, you need not answer this question.)

9. Did you or do you feel isolated or different from others? If so, how does that affect your life?

10. Have you ever felt or do you currently feel emotionally overwhelmed? How do you cope with this feeling?

11. Do you feel sexually confused, avoiding sex, or wanting sex all the time?

12. What are your initial feelings in completing this questionnaire and facing the reality or possibility of having been sexually abused?

13. Describe how you feel your abuse has affected your self-worth.

14. What are your fears about being involved in a sexual abuse support group?

15. What do you wish to accomplish in this group? What changes in yourself do you hope for?

Additional comments you would like to make:

INDICATIONS OF RECOVERY

As a victim progresses through recovery from sexual abuse, she should not ask herself, *"Will* the past continue to affect me?" but rather, *"How* will the past affect me?" Paul's approach to finding peace involved making his anxieties known to God (Phil. 4:6, 7). Such an exhortation implies the reality of anxiety and the necessity of being honest with God. Our hope in Christ focuses upon the Father's promise of a life to come without pain and suffering. Life this side of heaven will never be free from pain. Yet we can experience healing in this life as a foretaste of the life to come.

Recovery from the effects of sexual abuse does not follow a precise path. People's experiences and responses vary widely. Do not expect that you will simultaneously reach all fifteen of the goals listed here; rather, you may anticipate that you will have accomplished some before others are even well under way. But as you advance in your recovery from abuse, be assured that God will equip you with the ability to function in meeting life's inevitable challenges and surprises.

Remember, recovery is an ongoing process. Be honest in comparing your own behavior to the following characteristics of a recovered victim, but also be patient with yourself as you work toward the goals that are the most difficult for you.

1. She is willing to face the abuse and acknowledge the hurt and the pain.
2. She can express feelings and thoughts to significant others about the abuse.
3. She understands that she was a victim; that regardless of any consent she thinks she may have given, she was a victim.
4. She further understands that she was a victim of abuse regardless of any physical arousal she may have experienced.

5. She considers the abuse a violation and an evil.
6. She realizes the damage she experienced and has overcome personal feelings of shame and guilt.
7. She can identify her personal style of relating to others, including attempts to avert further hurt by avoiding honesty and intimacy.
8. She is able to overcome unrealistic fears and is not plagued with continued anxiety.
9. She understands that forgiveness does not require that she forget the experience.
10. She understands that to forgive the abuser is impossible apart from the experience of a deep understanding of God's forgiveness.
11. She has experienced an increase in her sense of worth as a person and is able to trust others.
12. She has the ability to have intimate relationships with spouse, family, and friends.
13. She is free from the burdens of perfectionism, of rage, of bitterness, and of depression.
14. She is able to have a healthy sexual relationship.
15. She has the ability to have a deep understanding and trusting relationship with God.

Part 2: Lessons for Group Study of *Beyond the Darkness*

Introduction

If you feel that you are qualified and capable of leading a group dealing directly with sexual abuse, you can begin the group by using the following 12 lessons. You may feel more comfortable doing your first teaching with a co-leader/facilitator who has had some teaching experience. If, however, as you begin to form your group, you or your church have any doubt about making it a sexual abuse group, begin with the *Search for Significance* materials and follow through with the materials for *Your Parents and You.*

If at any time you feel that you can no longer facilitate the group, for whatever reason, please allow at least one month for a new facilitator to take charge or for the group members to relocate to another in-progress group. Always remember that a major issue with sexual abuse victims is betrayal; consequently, seek whatever method of transition would least risk causing that feeling in the group members. Of course, if you are working with a co-facilitator, the transition is usually easier as members are already working with the individual who will remain with the group.

If you do choose to proceed with a study of *Beyond the Darkness,* it is recommended, because of the strong emotions aroused in dealing with sexual abuse, to prepare class members in advance for the possibility of going to an intermediate study before completing the series. Again, the issue of betrayal must be guarded against.

It is possible at any time in this series of 12 lessons that the emotions uncovered will be more explosive and overwhelming than you (and your co-facilitator, if present) are capable of handling. In that event, discontinue study of *Beyond the Darkness* and begin *The Search for Significance* series with your group. Follow this material with the lessons on *Codependency* and *Your Parents and You*. These three courses will provide helpful content in a positive environment so people in the group will be able to deal with the root issues of sexual abuse a bit more slowly. These lessons are much more direct in uncovering the pain and anger associated with sexual abuse.

If you encounter problems at any time for which you need assistance (remember, you do not want to position yourself as the rescuer for the group members), call the small group coordinator at your church or call Rapha's Support Group Facilitator's Hotline: 1-800-383-HOPE.

Lesson Goals

The goals of these lessons include:

1. Providing a stable, secure, and supportive environment which encourages openness and honesty.
2. Beginning to uncover the reality of hurt and pain, and to overcome denial.
3. Building strong relationships which provide the warmth, strength, and encouragement of the body of Christ.

Lesson Format

Each lesson plan for *Beyond the Darkness* is for a four-week period, and the complete set of 12 lessons is designed to cover the book and its workbook sections in approximately one year.

The format for the individual sessions includes:

An opening prayer. Many painful emotions and memories will be evoked during these lessons. Take some time to ask the Lord for His healing, comfort, and wisdom for people in the group.

Unison reading of help materials. This will consist of affirmations for restoration of group members' feelings of self-worth and self-esteem. Readings from *Beyond the Darkness* include "The Overcomer's Hopes," "God's Messages to You as a Believer," "God's Truths," and "Twelve Steps to Restoration."

Sharing. An opportunity is provided at the beginning of each group session for members to discuss any pressing needs. Members are not forced to speak if they are reluctant to do so.

Discussion of written assignment. Just before the closing prayer at each regular group session, members will have been assigned the task of making written responses to several of the questions in the workbook sections at the end of each chapter in *Beyond the Darkness.* During the next meeting, after the time for sharing, members will be asked to share their responses with the group. Don't insist that every individual share her responses; some may have given answers that are too personal for them to feel comfortable communicating to others. If they do not want to talk about their responses, you may want to share your own responses and then move on to the questions in the lesson.

Assignments. At this time, reading and workbook assignments are made for the next week's lesson. Also, information the members will need for the meeting can be announced.

Closing Prayer. Make this a time of praise for insights the Lord has brought during the meeting and for His help and support during the time until the group comes together again.

Planning for Your Group

As you plan your group activities, consider the following factors:

Group size and classtime duration. The group size and length of individual class sessions are determined by a number of factors. For example, the duration can vary from one to two hours. If the shorter time is found to be more advantageous for group members, the group size should not exceed five members. A recommended length of time is 90 minutes. Even with a two-hour class session, the group size should not exceed fifteen members. The recommended size is ten members.

Frequency of Meetings and Duration of Group. In school or hospital settings groups can meet from once a day to once a week. For self-help groups and for groups of incest victims a weekly meeting is probably most practical.

There are many possibilities as to the period of time the group will meet. Some groups meet for as short a period as six months, while others may meet for several years. It is recommended with the material to be covered in *Beyond the Darkness* that a year be established for the duration of the group. The longer period allows members to complete all the material suggested and also to deal with issues at a deeper level.

One of the major issues for any victim of abuse is a sense of worthlessness and low self-esteem. Completing the *Search for Significance* study, which is very helpful in dealing with that issue, takes 13 weeks for both book and workbook. Another major issue of sexual abuse is codependency. Completing the book *Codependency* in the group setting can also take 13 weeks. A third meaningful study, *Your Parents and You*, also lasts 13 weeks.

These additional books should be completed after *Beyond the Darkness* has been covered, unless they have already been undertaken. The order in which you present the content depends upon your experience and the needs of the members of your group.

Open and Closed Groups. An open system allows members to leave and new members to join the group so that the group has a changing membership. A closed group is one that starts with certain members and does not allow new members until the agreed duration of the group is completed.

There are advantages, disadvantages, and variations to

both group systems. A local church in Houston announces in their bulletin every three months the information on their sexual abuse group. For several Sundays the church encourages women to participate in the group. Each time new women are added to the group, and others leave. This group has been in existence for eighteen months. Some of the original members still participate in the group.

If more than fifteen need to participate, as may happen in large churches, several groups may be started. It is suggested that an open system be adopted with variations that will fit the needs of the members and the leaders.

Flexibility and Completeness. These lessons are designed to be completed in one year. However, you should feel free to spend more than the suggested time of one week on a lesson. For example, the members may wish to take an additional week to talk about the issues of guilt or anger. Exercise sensitivity and flexibility in your leadership as you help them complete the content, but do complete it.

Punctuality. Ending at a specific time is just as important as starting on time. If the session is supposed to end at a specific time, *do not go past that time!* It is better to have a lively discussion and end on time—even before finishing the material—than to go overtime with people wishing you had stopped. If you stop on time, those who need to leave can do so without embarrassment, and those who want to talk further can stay for awhile.

If you see that you will not have time to complete the questions before the end of the time, select particular questions which seem most important to the group and focus on them. You might also save time by going through the questions with the group without taking time to have them respond individually. The lack of individual reflection, however, may not allow people to wrestle deeply enough with the issues. As group leader, your role is to balance the depth of reflection, length of interaction, and time.

After Completing These Lessons

When your group has completed the lessons in this guide, please act on the suggestion made earlier to take them through the lessons for *The Search for Significance, Codependency,* and *Your Parents and You,* unless these have previously been undertaken. These materials are designed to help people apply scriptural principles to important aspects of their lives, such as: self-worth, the concept of God, forgiveness, and the formation of healthy relationships.

A small group leader's guide is available to help you lead your group through a 13-week study of each book. Books, workbooks, and leaders' guides for each series may be ordered from Rapha Publishing at 1-800-383-HOPE.

STUDY GUIDE

LESSON I
Chapters 1, 2, 3

Week 1

Step 1. Opening prayer.

Step 2. Discuss the format of the group—its size, its requirements for providing privacy, and its goals, as described in the early part of the Appendix.

Step 3. Review the symptoms of victims of abuse given in chapters 1 and 2 of *Beyond the Darkness*.
Open discussion on Job 30:26, asking members to describe what the verse means to them.

Step 4. Assign reading of chapters 1-3 and the workbook section of chapter 1. Ask members to write answers to the ten items at the end of chapter 1 and to be prepared to discuss material.

Step 5. Ending prayer.

Week 2

Step 1. Opening prayer.

Step 2. At the beginning of the meeting, give each member of the group an opportunity to discuss any pressing need. Make certain every person has the opportunity to speak, but do not force anyone to speak who is reluctant to do so.

Step 3. Begin to discuss the material that was assigned. It is suggested that members share all or a part of their assignment with the other members. It is also recommended that every member read her autobiography to the group. This is a very helpful way to learn about each other and begin the road to intimacy.

Step 4. Assign the workbook section of chapter 3 of *Beyond the Darkness*.

Step 5. Closing prayer.

257

Week 3

Step 1. Opening prayer.

Step 2. Read aloud, in unison, "The Overcomer's Hopes," p. 38 in *Beyond the Darkness.*

Step 3. Repeat step 2 of week 2, lesson 1.

Step 4. Open discussion of assigned material.

Step 5. Complete any unanswered material from the workbook sections of chapters 1 and 3 of *Beyond the Darkness* (pp. 10–12 and 39–41)

Step 6. Closing prayer.

Week 4

Step 1. Opening prayer

Step 2. Read aloud, in unison, "The Overcomer's Hopes," p. 38 in B*eyond the Darkness.*

Step 3. Repeat step 2 of week 2, lesson 1.

Step 4. Complete discussion of chapters 1, 2, and 3.

Step 5. Assignment: Read chapter 4 and do items 1, 2, and 3 from the workbook section on p. 55.

Step 6. Closing prayer.

LESSON 2
Chapter 4

Week 1

Step 1. Opening prayer.

Step 2. Read aloud, in unison, "God's Messages to You as a Believer" (*Beyond the Darkness*, p. 54).

Step 3. Repeat step 2 of week 2, lesson 1.

Step 4. Open discussion on items 1, 2, and 3 from the workbook section on p. 55.

Step 5. Assign workbook items 4, 5, 6, and 7, pp. 56–57 of *Beyond the Darkness.*

Step 6. Closing prayer.

Week 2

Step 1. Opening prayer.

Step 2. Read aloud, in unison, "God's Messages to You as a Believer" (*Beyond the Darkness*, p. 54).

Step 3. Repeat step 2 of week 2, lesson 1.

Step 4. Open discussion on items 4, 5, 6, and 7 from the workbook section on pp. 56–57.

Step 5. Assignment: Items 8, 9, and 10 of workbook section on p. 57 of *Beyond the Darkness*.

Step 6. Closing prayer.

Week 3

Step 1. Opening prayer.

Step 2. Read aloud, in unison, "God's Messages to You as a Believer" (*Beyond the Darkness*, p. 54).

Step 3. Repeat step 2 of week 2, lesson 1.

Step 4. Open discussion on items 8, 9, and 10 from the workbook section on p. 57 of *Beyond the Darkness*.

Step 5. Assignment: Review lesson 2 or complete any lesson 2 material that has not been finished.

Step 6. Closing prayer.

Week 4

Step 1. Opening prayer.

Step 2. Read aloud, in unison, "God's Messages to You as a Believer" (*Beyond the Darkness*, p. 54).

Step 3. Repeat step 2 of week 2, lesson 1.

Step 4. Open discussion on any material that has been assigned.

Step 5. Assignment: Read chapter 5 and complete items 1–5 from the workbook section on pp. 72–73 of *Beyond the Darkness*.

Step 6. Closing prayer.

LESSON 3
Chapters 5 and 6

Week 1

Step 1. Opening prayer.

Step 2. Read aloud, in unison, "God's Truths" (*Beyond the Darkness*, pp. 69–70).

Step 3. Repeat step 2 of week 2, lesson 1.

Step 4. Open discussion on items 1–5 from the workbook section on pp. 72–73.

Step 5. Assignment: Write answers to items 6–10 from the workbook section pp. 73–75.

Step 6. Closing prayer.

Week 2

Step 1. Opening prayer.

Step 2. Read aloud, in unison, "God's Truths" (*Beyond the Darkness*, pp. 69–70).

Step 3. Repeat step 2 of week 2, lesson 1.

Step 4. Open discussion on items 6–10 from the workbook section on pp. 73–75.

Step 5. Assignment: Read chapter 6 and write answers to items 1–5 from the workbook section on pp. 87–88.

Step 6. Pray the Prayer of Perseverance (p. 68, *Beyond the Darkness*) in unison.

Step 7. Closing prayer.

Week 3

Step 1. Opening prayer.

Step 2. Read aloud, in unison, "God's Truths" (*Beyond the Darkness*, pp. 69–70).

Step 3. Repeat step 2 of week 2, lesson 1.

Step 4. Open discussion on chapter 6 and items 1–5 from the workbook section on pp. 87–88.

Step 5. Assignment: Write answers to items 6–10 from the workbook section on pp. 88–89.

Step 6. Pray the Prayer of Perseverance (p. 68 of *Beyond the Darkness*) in unison.

Step 7. Closing prayer.

Week 4

Step 1. Opening prayer.

Step 2. Read aloud, in unison, "God's Truths" (*Beyond the Darkness*, pp. 69–70).

Step 3. Repeat step 2 of week 2, lesson 1.

Step 4. Complete discussion of chapter 6 and items 6–10 from the workbook section on pp. 88–89.

Step 5. Assignment: Read chapter 7 and write answers to items 1–3 from the workbook section on p. 98.

Step 6. Pray the Prayer of Perseverance (p. 68 of *Beyond the Darkness*) in unison.

Step 7. Closing prayer.

LESSON 4
Chapter 7

Week 1

Step 1. Opening prayer.

Step 2. Read aloud, in unison, "Twelve Steps to Restoration" (*Beyond the Darkness*, pp. 96–97).

Step 3. Repeat step 2 of week 2, lesson 1.

Step 4. Open discussion of chapter 7 and items 1–3 from the workbook section on p. 98.

Step 5. Assignment: Read Psalm 23 five times a day for the next week, write answers to items 4–6 from the workbook section on p. 99.

Step 6. Closing prayer.

Week 2

Step 1. Opening prayer.

Step 2. Read aloud, in unison, Psalm 23 (*Beyond the Darkness*, p. 94).

Step 3. Repeat step 2 of week 2, lesson 1.

Step 4. Continue discussion of chapter 7 and items 4–6 from the workbook section on p. 99.

Step 5. Assignment: Complete items 7–10 from the workbook section on pp. 99–100.

Step 6. Closing prayer.

Week 3

Step 1. Opening prayer.

Step 2. Repeat step 2 of week 2, lesson 1.

Step 3. Continue discussion of chapter 7 and items 7–10 from the workbook section on pp. 99–100.

Step 5. Assignment: Complete any unfinished material from chapter 7.

Step 6. Closing prayer.

Week 4

Step 1. Opening prayer.

Step 2. Read aloud, in unison, "Twelve Steps to Restoration" (*Beyond the Darkness*, pp. 96–97).

Step 3. Repeat step 2 of week 2, lesson 1.

Step 4. Complete discussion of chapter 7 and workbook section on pp. 98–100.

Step 5. Assignment: Read chapter 8, and complete workbook items 1–3, pp. 111–12.

Step 6. Pray Psalm 23 in unison.

Step 7. Closing prayer.

LESSON 5
Chapter 8

Week 1

Step 1. Opening prayer.

Step 2. Repeat step 2 of week 2, lesson 1.

Step 3. Discuss chapter 8 and workbook items 1–3 on pp. 111–12. Be sure to have members read and share their assignments.

Step 4. Assignment: Complete workbook items 4–7, pp. 112–13.

Step 5. Closing prayer.

Week 2

Step 1. Opening prayer.

Step 2. Repeat step 2 of week 2, lesson 1.

Step 3. Discuss chapter 8 and workbook items 4–7 on pp. 112–13.

Step 4. Assignment: Complete workbook items 8–10, p. 113.

Step 5. Closing prayer.

Week 3

Step 1. Opening prayer.

Step 2. Repeat step 2 of week 2, lesson 1.

Step 3. Continue discussion of chapter 8 and workbook items 8–10 on p. 113.

Step 4. Assignment: Complete any unfinished work on chapter 8.

Step 5. Closing prayer.

Week 4

Step 1. Opening prayer.

Step 2. Repeat step 2 of week 2, lesson 1.

Step 3. Complete discussion of chapter 8 and workbook section.

Step 4. Assignment: Read chapter 9 and complete workbook items 1–3, pp. 125–26.

Step 5. Closing prayer.

LESSON 6
Chapter 9

Week 1

Step 1. Opening prayer.

Step 2. Repeat step 2 of week 2, lesson 1.

Step 3. Discuss chapter 9 and workbook items 1–3, pp. 125–26.

Step 4. Assignment: Complete workbook items 4–7, pp. 126–27.

Step 5. Closing prayer.

Week 2

Step 1. Opening prayer.

Step 2. Repeat step 2 of week 2, lesson 1.

Step 3. Continue discussion of chapter 9 and workbook items 4–7, pp. 126–27.

Step 4. Assignment: Complete workbook items 8–10, p. 127.

Step 5. Closing prayer.

Week 3

Step 1. Opening prayer.

Step 2. Repeat step 2 of week 2, lesson 1.

Step 3. Continue discussion of chapter 9 and workbook items 8–10, p. 127.

Step 4. Assignment: Complete any unfinished material on chapter 9.

Step 5. Closing prayer.

Week 4

Step 1. Opening prayer.

Step 2. Repeat step 2 of week 2, lesson 1.

Step 3. Complete discussion of chapter 9 and any unfinished workbook items.

Step 4. Assignment: Read chapter 10 and do workbook items 1–3, p 139.

Step 5. Closing prayer.

LESSON 7
Chapter 10

Week 1

Step 1. Opening prayer.

Step 2. Repeat step 2 of week 2, lesson 1.

Step 3. Discuss chapter 10 and workbook items 1–3, p. 139.

Step 4. Assignment: Complete workbook items 4–7, pp. 140–41.

Step 5. Closing prayer.

Week 2

Step 1. Opening prayer.

Step 2. Repeat step 2 of week 2, lesson 1.

Step 3. Continue discussion of chapter 10 and workbook items 4–7, pp. 140–41.

Step 4. Assignment: Complete workbook items 8–10, p. 141.

Step 5. Closing prayer.

Week 3

Step 1. Opening prayer.

Step 2. Repeat step 2 of week 2, lesson 1.

Step 3. Continue discussing chapter 10 and workbook items 8–10, p. 141.

Step 4. Assignment: Complete all unfinished material from chapter 10.

Step 5. Closing prayer.

Week 4

Step 1. Opening prayer.

Step 2. Repeat step 2 of week 2, lesson 1.

Step 3. Complete discussion of chapter 10.

Step 4. Assignment: Read chapter 11 and do workbook items 1–3, p. 154.

Step 5. Closing prayer.

LESSON 8
Chapter 11

Week 1

Step 1. Opening prayer.

Step 2. Repeat step 2 of week 2, lesson 1.

Step 3. Begin discussion of chapter 11 and workbook items 1–3, p. 154.

Step 4. Assignment: Complete workbook items 4–7, pp. 154–55.

Step 5. Closing prayer.

Week 2

Step 1. Opening prayer.

Step 2. Repeat step 2 of week 2, lesson 1.

Step 3. Continue discussion of chapter 11 and workbook items 4–7, pp. 154–55.

Step 4. Assignment: Complete workbook items 8–10, pp. 155–56.

Step 5. Closing prayer.

Week 3

Step 1. Opening prayer.

Step 2. Repeat step 2 of week 2, lesson 1.

Step 3. Continue discussion of chapter 11 and workbook items 8–10, pp. 155–56.

Step 4. Assignment: Complete any unfinished material from chapter 11.

Step 5. Closing prayer.

Week 4

Step 1. Opening prayer.

Step 2. Repeat step 2 of week 2, lesson 1.

Step 3. Complete discussion of chapter 11 and all workbook items.

Step 4. Assignment: Read chapter 12 and do workbook items 1–3, p. 167.

Step 5. Closing prayer.

LESSON 9
Chapter 12

Week 1

Step 1. Opening prayer.

Step 2. Repeat step 2 of week 2, lesson 1.

Step 3. Begin discussion of chapter 12 and workbook items 1–3, p. 167.

Step 4. Assignment: Complete workbook items 4–7, pp. 168–69.

Step 5. Closing prayer.

Week 2

Step 1. Opening prayer.

Step 2. Repeat step 2 of week 2, lesson 1.

Step 3. Continue discussion of chapter 12 and workbook items 4–7, pp. 168–69.

Step 4. Assignment: Complete workbook items 8–10, p. 169.

Step 5. Closing prayer.

Week 3

Step 1. Opening prayer.

Step 2. Repeat step 2 of week 2, lesson 1.

Step 3. Continue discussion of chapter 12 and workbook items 8–10, p. 169.

Step 4. Assignment: Complete any unfinished material in chapter 12.

Step 5. Closing prayer.

Week 4

Step 1. Opening prayer.

Step 2. Repeat step 2 of week 2, lesson 1.

Step 3. Complete discussion of chapter 12 and all workbook items.

Step 4. Assignment: Read chapter 13 and do workbook items 1–3, p. 189.

Step 5. Closing prayer.

LESSON 10
Chapter 13

Week 1

Step 1. Opening prayer.

Step 2. Read in unison the Declaration and scriptures on pp. 176–77.

Step 3. Repeat step 2 of week 2, lesson 1.

Step 4. Begin discussion of chapter 13 and workbook items 1–3, p. 189.

Step 5. Assignment: Read daily the Declaration on p. 176. Complete workbook items 4–7, pp. 189–90.

Step 6. Closing prayer.

Week 2

Step 1. Opening prayer.

Step 2. Read in unison the Declaration and scriptures on pp. 176–77.

Step 3. Repeat step 2 of week 2, lesson 1.
Step 4. Continue discussion of chapter 13 and workbook items 4–7, pp. 189–90.
Step 5. Assignment: Read daily the Declaration on p. 176. Complete workbook items 8–10, p. 191.
Step 6. Closing prayer.

Week 3

Step 1. Opening prayer.
Step 2. Read in unison the Declaration and scriptures on pp. 176–77.
Step 3. Repeat step 2 of week 2, lesson 1.
Step 4. Continue discussion of chapter 13 and workbook items 8–10, p. 191.
Step 5. Assignment: Read daily the Declaration on p. 176. Complete any unfinished material from chapter 13.
Step 6. Closing prayer.

Week 4

Step 1. Opening prayer.
Step 2. Read in unison the Declaration and scriptures on pp. 176–77.
Step 3. Repeat step 2 of week 2, lesson 1.
Step 4. Complete discussion of chapter 13 and all workbook items.
Step 5. Assignment: Read chapter 14 and do workbook items 1–3, p. 212.
Step 6. Closing prayer.

LESSON 11
Chapter 14

Week 1

Step 1. Opening prayer.
Step 2. Read in unison the Declaration and scriptures on pp. 176–77.

Step 3. Repeat step 2 of week 2, lesson 1.
Step 4. Begin discussion of chapter 14 and workbook items 1–3, p. 212.
Step 5. Assignment: Read daily the Declaration on p. 176. Complete workbook items 4–7, pp. 212–13.
Step 6. Closing prayer.

Week 2
Step 1. Opening prayer.
Step 2. Read in unison the Declaration and scriptures on pp. 176–77.
Step 3. Repeat step 2 of week 2, lesson 1.
Step 4. Continue discussion of chapter 14 and workbook items 4–7, pp. 212–13.
Step 5. Assignment: Read daily the Declaration on p. 176. Complete workbook items 8–10, p. 214.
Step 6. Closing prayer.

Week 3
Step 1. Opening prayer.
Step 2. Read in unison the Declaration and scriptures on pp. 176–77.
Step 3. Repeat step 2 of week 2, lesson 1.
Step 4. Continue discussion of chapter 13 and workbook items 8–10, p. 214.
Step 5. Assignment: Read daily the Declaration on p. 176. Complete any unfinished material from chapter 14.
Step 6. Closing prayer.

Week 4
Step 1. Opening prayer.
Step 2. Read in unison the Declaration and scriptures on pp. 176–77.
Step 3. Repeat step 2 of week 2, lesson 1.

Step 4. Complete discussion of chapter 14 and all workbook items.

Step 5. Assignment: Read chapter 15 and do workbook items 1–3, p. 221.

Step 6. Closing prayer.

LESSON 12
Chapter 15

Week 1

Step 1. Opening prayer.

Step 2. Read in unison the Declaration and scriptures on pp. 176–77.

Step 3. Repeat step 2 of week 2, lesson 1.

Step 4. Begin discussion of chapter 15 and workbook items 1–3, p. 221.

Step 5. Assignment: Read daily the Declaration on p. 176. Complete workbook items 4–7, pp. 222–23.

Step 6. Closing prayer.

Week 2

Step 1. Opening prayer.

Step 2. Read in unison the Declaration and scriptures on pp. 176–77.

Step 3. Repeat step 2 of week 2, lesson 1.

Step 4. Continue discussion of chapter 14 and workbook items 4–7, pp. 222–23.

Step 5. Assignment: Read daily the Declaration on p. 176. Complete workbook items 8–10, p. 223.

Step 6. Closing prayer.

Week 3

Step 1. Opening prayer.

Step 2. Read in unison the Declaration and scriptures on pp. 176–77.

Step 3. Repeat step 2 of week 2, lesson 1.

Step 4. Continue discussion of chapter 15 and workbook items 8–10, p. 223.

Step 5. Assignment: Read daily the Declaration on p. 176. Complete any unfinished material from chapter 15.

Step 6. Closing prayer.

Week 4

Step 1. Opening prayer.

Step 2. Read in unison the Declaration and scriptures on pp. 176–77.

Step 3. Repeat step 2 of week 2, lesson 1.

Step 4. Complete discussion of chapter 15 and all workbook items.

Step 5. Closing prayer.

WORD ASSOCIATION QUIZ #1
(to be used with Chapter 4 Workbook questions)

DIRECTIONS:
As you read each word in column 1, fill in the corresponding blank in column 2 with the *first* word that comes into your mind.

1. mother   1. _____

2. mommy   2. _____

3. mom   3. _____

4. father   4. _____

5. daddy   5. _____

6. dad   6. _____

7. brother   7. _____

8. sister   8. _____

9. child   9. _____

10. boy   10. _____

11. girl   11. _____

12. baby   12. _____

13. aunt   13. _____

14. uncle   14. _____

15. cousin

16. man

17. woman

18. grandmother

19. grandfather

20. family

21. son

22. daughter

23. wife

24. husband

25. teenager

26. adult

27. stranger

28. neighbor

29. friend

30. God

15. _____

16. _____

17. _____

18. _____

19. _____

20. _____

21. _____

22. _____

23. _____

24. _____

25. _____

26. _____

27. _____

28. _____

29. _____

30. _____

WORD ASSOCIATION QUIZ #2
(to be used with Chapter 4 Workbook questions)

DIRECTIONS:
As you read each word in column 1, fill in the corresponding blank in column 2 with the *first* word that comes into your mind.

1. love

2. hate

3. confusion

4. mercy

5. jealousy

6. rejection

7. hope

8. fear

9. anger

10. weak

11. abandonment

12. loneliness

13. guilt

14. trust

1. _____

2. _____

3. _____

4. _____

5. _____

6. _____

7. _____

8. _____

9. _____

10. _____

11. _____

12. _____

13. _____

14. _____

15. life   15. _____

16. peace   16. _____

17. sin   17. _____

18. funny   18. _____

19. dream   19. _____

20. pain   20. _____

21. hurt   21. _____

22. sad   22. _____

23. betray   23. _____

24. shame   24. _____

25. important   25. _____

26. approval   26. _____

27. anxious   27. _____

28. helpless   28. _____

29. punish   29. _____

30. sex   30. _____